TUNING IN TO SAFETY

TUNING IN TO SAFETY

preparing your mind for the safety message

Tony Martin

ISBN: 1505417996
ISBN 13: 9781505417999
Library of Congress Control Number: 2017916726
CreateSpace Independent Publishing Platform
North Charleston, South Carolina

Table of Contents

Acknowledgments · vii
Foreword · xi

1   How this book can help you · · · · · · · · · · · · · · · · · 1
2   Production vs Safety · 7
3   Am I my brother's keeper? · · · · · · · · · · · · · · · · · ·21
4   Learning safety ·32
5   Delivering the message · · · · · · · · · · · · · · · · · · · 44
6   Receiving the message · 58
7   Enhancing your safety image · · · · · · · · · · · · · · · · 71
8   A self-imposed sense of urgency · · · · · · · · · · · · · · 85
9   Hierarchies · 100
10 Combating complacency · · · · · · · · · · · · · · · · · · ·113
11 Why supervisors die ·131
12 Counting the costs ·145

Ten Principles of Safety ·157
Endnotes ·159
About the Author ·161

Acknowledgments

I first had the idea for this book in summer of 2014. However, it took more than a year of careful thought and talking with friends and colleagues before I was able to put "pen to paper." While I have done a fair bit of writing over the past 14 years, I must admit that I am not prolific by any stretch of the imagination. My production is often in direct proportion to prodding and encouragement from those that are closest to me, and this project was no exception.

My friend Sean Bennett was one of the first individuals I talked to about my idea, and he was the one that said "write it before someone else does!" That was enough to catalyze me to get started, and Sean has been a writing accountability partner all the way through. The first six chapters were the most difficult because it still wasn't clear to me how the finished product was supposed to look. During that time, Sean kept nudging me and helping me see a dim light at the end of the tunnel. His editing ability stabilized the entire process because he thought carefully about what he was reading and may have seen the big picture better than I did. He was also kind enough to write the Foreword for this book, and I owe him a debt of gratitude for all his efforts.

A number of others were big encouragements to me as I wove my way through the project. Bill Whitmore recognized the vision of my idea early in the game and served as a sounding board as I put my thoughts into written form. Richard Long read all the chapters and made written suggestions on the ideas, as well as the grammar and organization of the content. Ryan Schmidt and I discussed much of the content of the book over a period of three years, and he helped gel my thinking and spur my production whenever I lost momentum.

I am also thankful for the family, friends, and colleagues who left their fingerprints on this book:

Tom Brice   Joanne Brindley
Don Burnett   Ragan Burns

Greg Chapin
Ethan Dabney
John Gentry
Celine Graas
JR Leckbee
Jacob A. Martin
Josiah A. Martin
Kathryn Martin
Tim Martin
Drew O'Brien
Roger Piek
Lance Sjostrand
Sean E. Smith
Sam Trotzke

Rick Cruea
Janice Fefchak
Stuart Goldstein
Colin Hendry
Richard Logan
John E. Martin
Joshua A. Martin
Kelly R. Martin
Clint Nebeker
Debbie Parrott
Erin Saari
Jamey E. Smith
Lawrence Sullivan

Above all, I thank my wife, Lara. From the opening days of this project, she understood the spirit of what I was trying to communicate and acted as a literary shepherd when I needed it most. She is an answer to prayer, my helpmeet, and the love of my life.

Foreword

A few years ago, I overheard a discussion on the subject of teaching safety that took place between two instructors of motive power technology in a vocational college staff room … it went something like this:

"I hate being assigned to teach safety modules to entry-level students. How do you go about teaching safety to twenty-year-olds, most of whom have never been injured and imagine they've been blessed with some kind of divine immunity to accidents?"

His colleague chuckled, "If you think that's tough, try doing it with a bunch of seasoned workers in a mostly male workplace in which strict adherence to safety regulations is viewed as being insufficiently macho."

Take a look at any set of safety guidelines, whether they are a component of a college curriculum or company policy initiatives, and they seldom make for compelling reading. To teach adults anything, there must be learner buy-in, a *what's in it for me* factor, and historically this has been a challenge when it comes to developing strategies for implementing workplace safety in occupations that have a higher potential for accidents. Some of the reasons for this are embedded in our culture; it is, after all, natural for us to admire the fireman who risks life and limb to effect a daring rescue from a burning building. But the harsh reality is that an avoidable workplace injury results in inevitable consequences for the worker, the victim's family, coworkers, and employer.

Tony Martin takes a holistic view of safety. His unique approach introduces his readers to the hard truths of safety malpractices from both an employer and employee perspective. Most important, he does not shy away from the seldom-mentioned realities of common shortcomings in safe work practice. In one chapter that I consider to be especially relevant, the tricky issue of the "safety culture" of the workplace is addressed head-on, dispelling myths surrounding some of the behaviors that prevail in a primarily male workforce. The book outlines in stark detail the human and financial tolls of safety infractions, drawing the reader into its message by using an appealing anecdotal approach.

At the core of this book's message is the author's experience of worker safety education in the mining industry. Its strength is in examining the challenges of ensuring that safety awareness is paramount in minds of both managers and employees, while never losing sight of the fact that the goal of any industrial operation is to make a profit. Tony cites a wide range of workplace safety issues using real-world examples and his solutions are not to condemn, but rather to be thoughtfully remedial.

By abandoning the tedious recital of regulations used in most safety literature, this book is innovative because it invites the reader to engage in the dialogue of safety strategies. Its use of everyday language and scenarios ensures that it entertains as well as educates. In addition to powerfully communicating the safety message to workers, it should also help the instructor I quoted at the beginning of this preface, to make his safety classes directed at entry level students more appealing.

Sean Bennett, Cengage Learning, Clifton Park, NY,
September 2017

How this book can help you

While some occupations are certainly more risky than others, everyone has the potential to get hurt while at work. Whether your job involves working at a computer, stocking shelves at a retail store, or operating heavy equipment, this book is for you.

Over the past several decades, the issue of workplace safety has gained momentum to become the predominant concern in industry. It wasn't that long ago that an injury at work, while certainly not desired, was an inconvenience at worst. Things have changed mightily since that time, primarily because we've gained a greater understanding of the true cost of a workplace injury.

We live in a time where companies and organizations spend millions of dollars in an effort to improve their safety record. Safety committees are formed for individual departments, and incentive programs are created to give tangible rewards to those who embrace the established safety culture. Any incident that takes place is investigated thoroughly and root causes are determined. In turn, policies and procedures are revised and the workforce is then retrained to implement the changes. Clearly, the stakes are high for an employer to dedicate this level of resources to making sure the same incident does not take place again.

Work conditions in the industrial world were very different at the turn of the previous century. In his book *The Jungle,* Upton Sinclair tells the story of Jurgis Rudkus, a Lithuanian immigrant who goes to work at a steel mill in South Chicago in 1904:

> *In a week Jurgis got over his sense of helplessness and bewilderment in the rail mill. He learned to find his way about and to take all the miracles and terrors for granted, to work without hearing the rumbling and crashing. From blind fear he went to the other extreme; he became reckless and indifferent, like all the rest of the men, who took but little thought of themselves in the ardor of their work. It was wonderful, when one*

came to think of it, that these men should have taken an interest in the work they did - they had no share in it - they were paid by the hour, and paid no more for being interested. Also they knew that if they were hurt they would be flung aside and forgotten - and they would still hurry to their task by dangerous short cuts, would use methods that were quicker and more effective in spite of the fact that they were also risky.

His fourth day at work Jurgis saw a man stumble while running in front of a car, and have his foot mashed off, and before he had been there three weeks he was witness of a yet more dreadful accident. There was a row of brick furnaces, shining white through every crack with the molten steel inside. Some of these were bulging dangerously, yet men worked before them, wearing blue glasses when they opened and shut the doors. One morning as Jurgis was passing, a furnace blew out, spraying two men with a shower of liquid fire. As they lay screaming and rolling upon the ground in agony, Jurgis rushed to help them, and as a result he lost a good part of the skin from the inside of one of his hands. The company doctor bandaged it up, but he got no other thanks from anyone, and was laid up for eight working days without any pay.[1]

The men at the steel mill were being paid by the hour and would receive no additional compensation for taking short-cuts. Their peril was heightened by the fact that in their day there was no such thing as Workers Compensation to fall back on if they did get hurt. The only explanation for their reckless behavior would be that they may have been afraid of losing their jobs if they were deemed to be working too slow. Despite having very little to gain and everything to lose, the men were willing to accept exorbitant risks to get their jobs done.

Workplace conditions in the U.S. have changed dramatically since 1904. While the business world has undergone a major shift in thinking regarding safety, the modern worker has not necessarily followed suit. Many companies are now willing to pay their employees to stay safe, yet we continue to see workers exhibiting unsafe behavior, much like the men at the steel mill in South Chicago. The "million dollar question" is what causes modern day workers to put themselves and their coworkers at risk, despite the disincentives to do so.

Let's talk briefly about you and your goals. What is your primary goal when you come to work each day? Do you think, in so many words, that you intend to make it through the work day without injuring yourself or others?

Let's take it one step further. What is your ultimate goal in terms of your career? Some may say that long-term goals such as promotions or increased compensation would be of highest importance, but this might be overlooking something that could be far more important to you. How do you feel about going into retirement compromised by poor health due to workplace injuries? Safety rules seem like a hassle in the here and now, but will you regret taking the time to follow them when you enter your retirement years injury-free?

You've likely heard the saying that describes why small businesses often fail: "they didn't plan to fail, they failed to plan." While nobody plans on getting hurt on the job, employees often fail to make a plan on how to NOT hurt themselves or others. Safety policies and procedures can only go so far. In the end, it is the mindset of the individual employee that determines success or failure of a safety program.

A large number of workplace incidents are the result of poor decisions on the part of the employee. They often had adequate training and proper equipment at their disposal, yet they made a choice to act in an unsafe manner. Many of these decisions are made subconsciously, driven by personality type, emotions and assumptions. This book was written, in part, to encourage the reader to think introspectively. In other words, you are being asked to think about your thinking.

Some questions to ponder:

- What are your personal safety goals?
- Are your employer's safety goals different from your personal safety goals? If so, how?
- How does your thinking impact your ability to work safely?
- What role do you play in keeping your coworkers safe?
- How do you respond to your coworkers when they approach you with a safety concern?
- What will it cost you if you get injured?

The safety message is all around us, and the key to staying injury-free is to open your mind to hear it. This book is about "tuning in" to the safety message...and letting it change you, your behavior, and the very culture of your workplace.

Prepare to be challenged!

2

Production vs Safety

"Patience is bitter, but its fruit is sweet."

- JEAN-JACQUES ROUSSEAU

The classic struggle in industry is production versus safety. Everyone knows that production pays the bills and keeps us all employed. If we don't get the job done, surely our employer will go broke. Safety, on the other hand, is often thought of as being the polar opposite of production. The more we focus on being safe, the less we will produce and the less money our employer will make.

If there was a time that this thinking was valid, that time is gone.

There was a time when production was the only real concern in industry, and incidents were little more than an inconvenience. The financial impact of an incident was relatively minimal, and thus they were considered to be a normal cost of doing business. The bottom line, so to speak, was that incidents didn't have a major impact on the bottom line. Nobody was trying to get people hurt on the job, but at the same time there was little effort being made to prevent injuries. While some of us have been around long enough to remember those days, none would wish to go back.

Pause for a moment and read the next sentence slowly and carefully. *Incidents have a much greater financial impact than whatever production is lost in an effort to be safe.*

Did you catch that? We may all nod our heads dutifully when we read it, but deep down we don't believe it. Even worse, we often act out our disbelief by continuing to take inappropriate risks while on the job. We then justify our unsafe behavior by thinking that we are doing our employer a favor.

Your thinking may change if you are made aware of the true costs of an incident, which involves both direct and indirect costs. Direct costs include replacement wages for the worker, as well as medical expenses such as hospitalization, surgeries, prescriptions, and physical rehabilitation. This could also involve a long-term disability benefit or lump sum settlement if the worker suffers a permanent injury. While the direct costs of an incident can be significant, they still only represent one element of the total cost incurred.

INDIRECT COSTS

What many people fail to consider are the hidden costs, more commonly known as *indirect costs*. The indirect costs of an incident are cascading liabilities. In other words, an increase in one often creates a ripple effect, causing others to grow as well. There is a long list of indirect costs, a number of which are summarized below:

Wages and training for replacement workers. An injured worker oftentimes cannot function in their normal role until they are fully recovered. In the meantime, their workload is often distributed to existing employees, which may increase overtime wage costs. While this is the simplest approach, it can also serve to increase stress and fatigue, making it more likely that another incident will occur.

An alternative is to hire replacements to perform the duties of the injured worker. This is also a drag on the operation as the replacement worker requires training and supervision from other experienced workers. While the injured employee is often drawing disability benefits, the replacement employee has to be paid too.

Productivity lost due to reduced employee morale and increased absenteeism. The effectiveness of an institutional safety program is easy to quantify; if people are getting hurt, the safety program isn't working. Furthermore, everyone else starts wondering when it will be their turn. The overall effect is a reduction in morale and fewer reasons to come to work each day. Employees use up their sick leave and may start looking for a new job.

The work still has to be done even if some of the people aren't there to help. Those who do come to work are then tasked with doing the jobs of those who didn't show that day. This increase in workload contributes to a further decrease in morale.

It's easy to see the negative effect that this has on other indirect costs. Certainly, employee recruitment becomes that much more difficult (and expensive) under these

conditions, along with an associated increase in administrative costs.

**Repair and/or replacement of damaged property and
equipment.** An incident that leads to property or equipment
damage can result in significant costs, even if nobody got hurt.
However, the immediate costs are only one factor here. When
equipment gets damaged, it is out of commission until it is
repaired or replaced. This contributes to a loss of production
and adds to the workload of those who are tasked with performing the repair. Equipment that is critical to the business
will incur even greater repair costs because of expedited freight
charges for parts and other emergency costs.

If the machine is damaged to the point where it must
be replaced, the new machine may be different from the
original. If so, new procedures may have to be established
and retraining could be required for those who will oper-
ate the machine as well as those who are responsible for its
maintenance and repair. Spare parts may have to be put
into inventory, and parts from the old machine removed
and discarded.

Administrative overhead. Incidents are a trigger for
a proverbial avalanche of paperwork. Every company will

have different internal policies, but regardless there will be forms to be filled out and filed appropriately. In many cases, paperwork also has to be filed with government agencies such as OSHA (Occupational Safety and Health Administration) or MSHA (Mine Safety and Health Administration). All of this takes time and energy on the part of the administrative staff, resources that could be put to work in ways that actually make the company money.

Expenses related to increased regulatory oversight. Regulatory agencies such as OSHA and MSHA tend to focus their attention on companies or work sites where incidents have taken place in the past. This increases frequency and intensity of site visits, as well as the likelihood of additional citations and fines.

Productivity lost due to incident investigation and company policy reform. Incidents don't just happen and then go away, they tend to take on a life of their own. Typically, an internal investigation is conducted in an effort to determine root causes, then policies are reviewed in light of the new information. If a policy requires revision, a process of rewriting and review is undertaken, usually involving numerous people from the affected department. The revised policy is then put into motion, which could be as simple as posting it on the company website all the way up to retraining for thousands of employees.

Increases in insurance costs. Like any other industry, an insurance company's business model is built on limiting its exposure to risk. A company with a good safety record is less likely to file claims and is thus charged lower rates for its insurance coverage. The exact opposite happens when incidents take place. When risk increases, insurance rates skyrocket.

The direct costs of an incident are often recoverable through a Workers Compensation claim, but this will result in an increase of the premiums that the company pays for their coverage. Workers Compensation insurance is expensive to begin with, but will cost that much more for a company with a poor safety record. A rate increase brought on by an incident and an associated claim typically remains effective for three years, representing a significant long-term expense to the business.

Loss of competitive ability. Incident-related expenses inflict serious damage to a company's profitability, making it that much more difficult to compete for new business. A poor safety record can also disqualify a company from bidding on contracts because they are viewed as a liability by their peers. Other businesses don't want to be associated with a company that doesn't perform well on the safety front because they fear it will cost them their reputation and ability to compete.

Environmental liabilities.   Safety incidents can also result in expenses related to environmental calamities. A glaring example of this is the explosion and fire aboard the Deepwater Horizon, an offshore oil drilling rig in the Gulf of Mexico. Along with the loss of 11 lives, millions of gallons of crude oil were spilled in the Gulf. This catastrophe has cost BP tens of billions of dollars and caused a near-collapse of the company.

Erosion of company image in the eyes of the public, impacting both sales and recruiting. Public image is everything in the world of business. A quick path for a company to ruin its image is to make a habit of getting people hurt. Employee recruitment is challenging enough as it is, but gains another level of difficulty due to people not wanting to work for a company with a poor safety record. Beyond that, people don't feel compelled to buy products from a company that is perceived to have little regard for the safety of its employees.

A company that is known to be a safe place to work has a much easier time selling their products and recruiting employees. While incidents set a series of cascading liabilities into motion, an excellent safety record only pays dividends.

ADDING IT UP

To fully appreciate the role that safety plays in a modern company's business model, one must be able to see the big picture. Where safety was once viewed as an isolated expense on a balance sheet, it now permeates all aspects of many company's operations. The business world has experienced a true paradigm shift; instead of safety counteracting production, it now goes hand-in-hand with production. At the end of the day, we will all make more money when we work safely.

This transformation has been catalyzed, in no small part, by the crushing financial impact of incidents. In order to provide information on these costs to small businesses, OSHA has developed $afety Pays, an estimating tool that is available on the *osha.gov* website.[2] According to OSHA, the ratio of the indirect costs of an incident to the direct costs can go as high as 4.5:1. Generally speaking, an incident with a lower direct cost will result in a higher ratio of indirect costs to direct costs.

For example, a relatively minor incident with direct costs of up to $2999 will have a ratio of 4.5:1.

Direct costs = $2000
Indirect costs (direct costs x 4.5) = $9000
Total (direct + indirect costs) = $11,000

However, an incident with direct costs of $10,000 or more will have a ratio of 1.1:1.

Direct costs = $50,000
Indirect costs (direct costs x 1.1) = $55,000
Total (direct + indirect costs) = $105,000

The $afety Pays estimator also calculates the amount of additional revenue the company would need to generate in order to cover the cost of the incident. Assuming that the direct costs of $50,000 are paid by insurance and the company has a profit margin of 3%, it will take $1,833,333 of additional revenue to make up indirect costs of $55,000. When it is expressed in those terms, any reasonable person will agree that money spent on preventing incidents can pay back many times over.

RIDING FOR THE BRAND

The true cost of incidents is fully understood by business leaders around the world. They have learned that a company performs better if its workforce stops taking inappropriate risks to meet production goals. However, there is a communication breakdown taking place, and despite the employer's best efforts, the employees aren't always getting the message. This is a never-ending source of frustration to the CEOs and CFOs of the world's biggest companies. What is it that makes our people take risks, when we keep telling them not to?

The modern worker's willingness to take risks to get the job done is sometimes deep-rooted, reinforced by generational expectations. Our ancestors lived at a time when production was the only thing anyone cared about. If you didn't produce, you would be replaced with someone who would. Injuries were considered to be a "Red Badge of Courage." If you were working like you were supposed to, it was natural to expect that you would get hurt from time to time. This mindset is best described by a phrase coined in the American Old West, "Ride for the Brand." Any cowboy working for a ranch was expected to do whatever was necessary to get the day's work done. He would work harder, stay on the job longer, and even put himself at risk for the sake of the ranch. Yes, he was riding for the brand, but he was also putting it on the line for his brothers in arms, the other cowboys at the ranch. Even more important, it was paying respect to his forefathers, acknowledging the sacrifices they had made and pledging that he was willing to do the same.

Times have changed. The ranch has concluded that the costs of getting cowboys hurt are unacceptable, and they want them to stop putting themselves at risk. However, the cowboys are often doing what their fathers and grandfathers did, behaviors steeped in honor and pride. Mindsets such as these won't be changed overnight.

Years ago, I was hired by an oilfield contracting company to do gas turbine inspections during an annual shutdown at a natural gas processing plant in Southcentral Alaska. I was one of several dozen workers that were brought in to help the regular employees perform major maintenance at the plant.

For the most part, the men that were hired were in their 20s or 30s, but there was one gentleman in his 60s that was brought in as a laborer. Once the project got underway, he immediately developed a reputation as being someone who would outwork everyone on his crew. He would lift more, carry more, and work faster than anyone else, which made the younger men wonder what he was trying to prove. While they admired his work ethic, they didn't think much of his tendency to take shortcuts. Everyone was being paid by the hour, and there wasn't going to be any rewards for those who assumed extra risk to get the job done.

Later that month, the project was slowly drawing to a close and individual jobs were being wrapped up one at a time. The laborer's crew was working at an area of the plant that was accessed using extension ladders, and as the job was finishing they started carrying their tools and equipment back down to the ground level. True to form, the laborer insisted on carrying more than anyone else on his crew, and was descending the ladders with heavier loads than he could safely handle. On one of his trips down, he lost his balance and fell from 10 feet up to the concrete below. He landed on his side and broke his arm and pelvis, putting him in the hospital and permanently altering his working career and personal life.

There are shortcuts that make perfect sense and don't increase risk to the worker. That is not the type of shortcut being discussed in this book. Shortcuts, for our purposes, are where a worker skips steps to save time and/or effort but increases the likelihood of getting hurt. In his mind, the laborer was "riding for the brand" when he carried more gear to reduce the number of trips he would have to take down the ladder. Unfortunately, his actions resulted in an incident that cost his employer tens of thousands of dollars and made it more difficult to compete for new business.

We sometimes justify unsafe behavior by telling ourselves that we are saving money for our employer. The reality is that the opposite is true...you are jeopardizing your employer, yourself, and your coworkers when you work in an unsafe manner.

Principle #1: You aren't doing yourself or your employer any favors when you take shortcuts.

Question to Consider: Do you believe that your employer is better off when you emphasize production over safety?

—⁄⁄⁄—

3

Am I my brother's keeper?

"True humility is not thinking less of yourself;
it is thinking of yourself less."

- C.S. Lewis

A common sight in the workplace is signs under the restroom mirrors with the words "You are looking at the person responsible for your safety." For the most part, there is little argument with this statement. A majority of workers recognize that they must assume responsibility for their actions, and they hold the key regarding whether they work safely or not.

Somewhat more controversial is the question of what responsibility the individual bears for the safety of their coworkers.

Society has taught us to look out for Number One. Nice guys finish last. It's a dog eat dog world. Deep down, we'd like to believe in the innate goodness of mankind, but life's lessons often serve to reinforce a cynical view of life and relationships. This same attitude can be carried over in our approach to safety in the workplace. Yes, I need to take care of myself, but that is where my responsibility ends.

The reality is that you cannot work safely without the help of your coworkers. In turn, your coworkers cannot work safely without you looking out for them. For the purposes of our discussion, there are three presuppositions we must affirm if we wish to create a safe workplace.

1. No one person can have enough information to always act safely.
2. Each and every one of your coworkers will have a different perspective and can be a source of valuable safety information.
3. Everyone bears responsibility for their coworker's safety. In other words, *you are your brother's keeper.*

The workplace environment is often very busy; many people performing dozens if not hundreds of tasks, sometimes independently and other times in groups. Many of the tasks being performed are not particularly risky, but others can have the potential for bad things to happen if care is not taken. In some cases, a task that is initially thought to be low-risk turns out to be very dangerous. Unfortunately, it is these types of tasks that often turn into incidents.

The flight deck of an aircraft carrier is an example of an extremely busy workplace environment. Jets taking off, jets landing, jets being prepared for their next mission, and hundreds of personnel performing their individual tasks to accomplish the overall mission of the carrier group. The noise level is such that communication is challenging at best; most tasks are performed using hand signals or radio communication. The potential for incidents to take place in this context is beyond comprehension.

The responsibility for all flight deck operations falls on the Air Officer, better known as the Air Boss. The Air Boss performs their duties from the primary flight control, located six stories up in the aircraft carrier's tower, or island. From this vantage point, they can maintain visual contact with all the activities taking place on the flight deck. The Air Boss can also see many things that personnel on the flight deck can't see, and it is their responsibility to ensure the safety of those same personnel.

Imagine a Sailor walking across the flight deck, completely unaware that they are about to step into the jet blast from a taxiing aircraft. From their own perspective, the Sailor is thinking that they are perfectly safe, but from high up in the primary flight control, the Air Boss can clearly see what is about to happen. The Sailor's ego will sting a little from the chewing out they receive, but they can be thankful that they weren't sent over the side of the ship because the Air Boss was watching out for their safety.

While each crewmember is trained to do everything they can to not get themselves or their fellow Sailors hurt, they are handicapped by a limited perspective. There are many people and too much going on for any one person on the flight deck to have enough information to always act safely. The Air Boss sees the situation from a "bird's eye view" and is ready to intervene if he sees something about to go awry.

Unfortunately, most workers do not have the benefit of an Air Boss watching over them while they perform their daily tasks. What they do have, however, is their coworkers, some of whom may be working alongside them on the same task or possibly observing from a distance.

Any one of us can find ourselves in a similar situation to the Sailor working on the flight deck of an aircraft carrier. When we concentrate on the task at hand, we can lose awareness of the bigger picture of activity around us. The situation can change quickly in a busy work environment; new tasks being undertaken, new equipment moving into the area, etc. Even the task we are working on can change without our being aware.

I know this to be true from personal experience. Early in my career, I was working on a crew that was installing a gas turbine engine on an offshore oil platform in Alaska's Cook Inlet. Our crew had taken the machine out earlier and shipped it to the shop for repair, and now we had returned with the rebuilt unit for installation.

Most of this project was fairly routine, except that we had removed a section of stainless steel tubing that was attached to the turbine's air intake and ran up and across the module we were working in. The open end of the tubing above us was never capped, and we didn't follow it or even care what it was for because it wasn't important to the task at hand. While the turbine install was taking place, the tubing was left aside as it would be one of the last pieces to be reattached.

The job continued over three days and, as time went on, there was progressively more activity happening nearby. We were joined by a welder who was working on some ducting that was also high up in the module. The welder had a hot work permit, which meant that the platform operators had checked our area for combustible gases and had deemed it to be safe for welding operations. Issuing a hot work permit also meant that they had disabled the fire detection system in our module. With the proper paperwork in hand, the welder then proceeded to arc weld on the steel ductwork above us while working from a ladder.

The work in our module continued until a gas turbine generator that was running in the adjacent module suddenly shut down. Within a couple minutes, one of the platform operators walked hurriedly through our area and stepped through a door that opened to the outside. What we didn't realize is that he was opening the valves on three large cylinders that were located outside our module. Moments later, propane gas started flowing into our module through the stainless steel tubing we had left uncapped. Worse yet, the welder had struck an arc and was actively welding when I and the other workers on our crew smelled the propane.

The welder had his mask down and was oblivious to what was going on around him as he welded on the ductwork. We all shouted for him to stop and scrambled outside to shut off the valves on the propane cylinders. Fortunately, we were able to get the welder to extinguish his arc in time. This prevented what could have been an explosion and fire, which would have been that much worse because the module's fire detection system had been disabled as part of the hot work permit.

It wasn't until we had experienced this near miss that we discovered the purpose of the stainless steel tubing that we had removed earlier. For some reason, gas turbine engines would not start on the natural gas that was produced on that platform. The only way the operators could get them to start was to enrich the intake air with propane, thus the propane cylinders and associated plumbing that ran to the air intakes of the turbines in these modules. We had removed a section of this tubing and left the end open, completely unaware of the potential danger.

The outcome would have been much different if the welder had been working by himself. Without me and the other workers looking out from below, there probably would have been an explosion and fire resulting in extensive damage and perhaps even loss of life. On the one hand, our crew had inadvertently caused the incident, but our perspective also prevented it from going beyond a near miss.

STRENGTH IN NUMBERS

There is strength in numbers when it comes to assessing hazards in the workplace. Each individual will look at the situation with a different set of eyes, and where one person sees no problem, another may have a completely different interpretation. Which would you prefer: working alone and having only your own senses to depend on to stay safe, or having multiple sets of eyes and ears looking out for your welfare? The answer is clear: two or more heads are better than one when it comes to safety. Keep in mind that this works best if everyone in the group is engaged in the exercise. A lack of focus on the part of one or more of the participants can jeopardize the process. Everyone needs to stay alert and keep their head in the game.

I know some heavy duty mechanics that were servicing a large articulating loader while its engine was running. One of the mechanics was in the operator's seat and another was working on the ground near the loader's articulation joint. For those who are unfamiliar, an articulating loader hinges at the machine center and is steered by using hydraulics to pivot itself from side to side. A safety feature on these machines is a steel connecting rod known as a steering frame lock that is installed to prevent the machine from steering while technicians work near the machine's articulation joint.

The steering frame lock was not installed at the time, and a visiting engineer happened to walk by as they ran the machine in the shop. The engineer was outraged when he saw what was happening. He yelled and told them to install the steering frame lock before any further work was done. While the mechanics knew they should have already done this, they didn't understand why the engineer was so emotional. What was the big deal?

As it turned out, the engineer had recently come from a shop that had suffered a grievous incident. One of his friends had been working near the articulation joint of a running loader, and the operator steered the machine in the direction that caught his friend in the pinch point and killed him. Little wonder that he was passionate about the issue. He saw the situation for what it was: the potential to cause a fatality.

This story illustrates the strength of having numerous individuals involved in hazard assessment. Each worker will have different priorities concerning hazards and will feel more strongly about those that caused them to suffer loss in the past. This can play in our favor if we are willing to learn from others, including those that are new to the industry.

We, in turn, must be willing to share our life experiences and have the moral courage to intervene in situations that we view as hazardous. There are many reasons why we hesitate to do this, but it gets easier when people understand that you are committed to their safety. The key is to start by listening to your coworkers and acknowledge the contribution that they are making to your own safety. In time, they will be willing to do the same for you.

Yes, you are your brother's keeper...but that same person may just save your life one day. We are all in this together.

—ɯɯ—

Principle #2: For your own sake,
you are your brother's keeper.

Question to Consider: Are you willing to speak
up when you see safety hazards in the workplace?

—ɯɯ—

4

Learning safety

"The great aim of education is not knowledge, but action."

- Herbert Spencer

Many companies commit a great deal of time and expense to the training and retraining of their workforce in safety policy and procedures. New hires often receive safety training before they begin their work duties. Existing employees are given regular refreshers and updates in an effort to nurture the company safety culture and keep incident rates down. While some of this training is driven by a need to comply with governmental regulations, most of it is voluntary on the part of the company because it makes good business sense. A safe workforce functions better no matter how you measure it, and can only make the company stronger.

The challenge is that teaching safety effectively is more difficult than it sounds. How much of what we teach actually turns into changed behavior? The ultimate goal of safety training is to help the employees become safer workers. However, we often assume that our teaching is much more effective than it actually is. We are far too reliant on PowerPoint and dispensing information orally, which allows the learner to disengage on an intellectual and emotional level. The consequence of this approach is that the student is left feeling that safety training is something to be endured, rather than helping them to function better in the workplace.

A factor that is often overlooked in adult learning is the role of human emotions in retaining and assimilating information. There is a good deal of educational research supporting the idea that deep learning does not take place until emotions are engaged. Put another way, adult learning becomes much more effective when the learner experiences anger, pain, fear, or embarrassment as part of the learning process. This is why the "school of hard knocks" is so powerful. Lessons learned the hard way are the ones that stick.

You know this to be true based on your personal experience. All of the lessons you have learned the best came about because your emotions were actively engaged when you experienced them. What lessons will you never forget? It will be those where you suffered loss at some level. The greater the loss, the deeper the lesson learned.

SAFETY KNOWLEDGE

For the purposes of our discussion, I propose that there are two types of safety knowledge: latent and active.

Latent safety knowledge is facts and principles that you remember on an intellectual level, but have minimal impact on your behavior. You don't think that the information applies to you, and you may not even believe it is true. Predictably, latent safety knowledge is a product of passive learning; the learner has little at stake and has difficulty seeing its relevance.

Active safety knowledge, in contrast, is highly relevant to you because you have established a personal connection with the information. Active safety knowledge could have been latent at one time, but has now gained importance due to a learning experience that engaged your emotions. This could involve an incident that you or someone close to you has experienced. The information is viewed in a different light and is now heartfelt, rather than just intellectual in nature.

A lesson I learned the hard way illustrates the difference between latent and active safety knowledge. I am a graduate of the Canadian Interprovincial Apprenticeship system, also known as the Red Seal program. My heavy duty equipment mechanic apprenticeship was set up to be four years in duration, with a total of 7200 hours served to graduate. Technical training was an integral part of the program, but it was relatively short in duration and took place once per year. The rest of the time, we apprentices learned our trade in the real world and got paid to do it.

During the technical training in the second year of my apprenticeship, our instructor told us that it was possible to cause an automotive battery to explode. We were told to avoid creating sparks around a lead-acid battery because they generate flammable hydrogen gas when they are charging. To prevent sparks from being created around a charging battery, we were told to turn off the charger and disconnect its power cord from the wall socket before removing the charging leads.

I remembered all of that information, probably because the idea of an exploding battery caught my attention. However, I didn't take any of it particularly seriously because I had never seen a battery explosion myself, and didn't know anyone that it had happened to. For all I knew, it may have been a myth. At this point, battery explosion prevention was latent safety knowledge and had very little influence on my behavior.

As my apprenticeship progressed into its third year, I was doing more work independently and trying hard to show the journeymen in the shop that I could "run with the big dogs." This meant taking the occasional shortcut, especially with jobs that I had done multiple times. What is strange about this is I was being paid by the hour, and there wasn't any financial incentive to get into a rush. My haste was primarily ego-driven; I was going to show the world that I could turn out the work as quickly as anyone.

I should also explain that the shops I worked in at the time did not emphasize the use of personal protective equipment (PPE). We did wear steel-toe boots, but everything else was optional. This included safety glasses; if you didn't feel like wearing them, nobody was going to give you a hassle. Without anyone saying it in so many words, you were considered to be weak if you wore them. Safety glasses were not provided by the company, and none of us felt strongly enough about our personal safety to invest in them either.

One task that I performed dozens of times was battery service. This involved cleaning, charging, testing, and replacing highway truck batteries, which lead a hard life and require frequent maintenance. While I never did it deliberately, I had created sparks around batteries before without incident. I have a combination wrench in my toolbox that will testify to this. The open end is melted in several places due to inadvertent contact between a battery positive terminal and ground. This only served to reinforce my skepticism that a lead-acid battery could explode. Consequently, my "fear factor" when I worked around batteries had dropped to zero so I never bothered wearing a face shield or safety glasses while I performed those tasks.

This all changed one day when I was tasked with servicing the batteries on an older farm truck. This particular truck had four batteries, and I disconnected all the cables before cleaning the posts, cable ends, and the tops of the batteries themselves. After everything was cleaned up, I reconnected all of the cables except the one that connects the battery negative to the vehicle frame. I then attached a battery charger and adjusted the setting to "high." The four batteries were now being fast-charged, and shortly thereafter I could detect the sulfur odor that indicates the batteries were gassing. As mentioned earlier, the gases being vented from a lead-acid battery contain hydrogen, which is odorless but highly explosive if allowed to accumulate.

I was in a hurry to get this truck wrapped up and out the door, but only because I was putting pressure on myself. My boss would have been satisfied to see the job done properly, and he wasn't putting any direct pressure on me to get it finished up. Instead of turning off the battery charger and disconnecting the charger leads before going to the next step, I attempted to make the final cable connection from the battery negative to the truck frame. I hesitated when I saw the connection spark when I first touched it, indicating that an electrical component on the truck was drawing power. I had made sparks like that around batteries before, but never while they were on the fast-charge.

I was conflicted. Seeing the spark had brought some latent safety knowledge to the forefront. I had created the conditions where a battery explosion could take place. While the voice of reason was telling me to shut off the battery charger and allow the gases to disperse before making the final connection, a competing voice was saying that this battery explosion thing is a fairy tale...get it done!

Without any further thought, I decided to push forward with connecting the batteries. I thrust the ground cable into place on the battery negative post, and BOOM! The battery I was connecting to exploded with my face directly over top of it. All at once I couldn't see anything, and my immediate thought was that my condition was permanent. I had been taught that this could happen, and due to my foolishness, I was now a blind man.

It is an understatement to say that my emotions were now engaged, and at the forefront was extraordinary anger with myself. There was also a feeling of intense embarrassment, as I knew better and had ignored the warnings I had received in the past. Past that, I was overwhelmed with fear when I considered the implications of being blind. How would I function from day-to-day, and how would I support myself? This business of battery explosions was no longer latent safety knowledge...it had been upgraded to active status. It was real.

I was taken to the local hospital's emergency room, and in time it became clear that I was not blind but my eyes had been burned in the explosion. Miraculously, none of the pieces of the battery case were lodged in my eyes. I was able to go home with ointment and gauze on both eyes and then return to work later that week. This is amazing when you consider that the entire top half of the battery case came apart when the explosion took place.

How did this experience change my behavior? Let's just say that I no longer looked at someone as if they were a wimp when they wore safety glasses. Later in my career, I taught college classes in automotive and diesel technology. If a student came into the lab without their safety glasses, I told him to put them on. If he wouldn't put them on, I told him to leave. Once, I had a student that was about to take the battery charger leads off a battery without shutting off the charger first. I yelled for him to stop. He did, but was visibly upset that I had raised my voice. I apologized for yelling, but told him that I had done him a favor because he could have caused a battery explosion. Clearly, my experience had left a mark and it was a lesson I would never forget.

This also helps explain the story of the mechanics running the articulating loader in the previous chapter. Why was the engineer so upset about someone working in the unlocked articulation joint of a running loader? Because he had seen someone killed doing that very thing. For the two mechanics, they knew better but this was latent safety knowledge and did little to change their behavior. The same information was active safety knowledge to the engineer, and he was going to make sure a similar incident didn't happen on his watch.

Incidents often change your thinking for the better. While it is the least desirable form of education, it is certainly the most effective. Anyone that has suffered the consequences of an incident has been promoted to a position of leadership. People sit up and pay attention when this person speaks on the subject. They are likely passionate about the issue and are much more willing to intervene if they see the same mistake being made again.

STRATEGIES FOR LEARNING SAFETY

The ultimate goal when teaching safety is to inspire your students to consistently model good safety practice. Filling their heads up with safety knowledge is not enough. We want the students to take the information to heart and use it to become safer workers.

Unfortunately, much of the safety information we have at our disposal is retained as latent safety knowledge. Workers sometimes lack the experience to know why the information is important and may conclude that it doesn't apply to them. In the most extreme scenario, an inexperienced employee could decide that the information isn't even true. These outcomes are the exact opposite of what we set out to accomplish.

No matter the quality of the safety training, every student needs to take responsibility for their own learning. This involves disciplining oneself to engage with the material and overcome the pitfalls of passive learning. Here are some strategies for anyone that wants to maximize the benefit they and their fellow students receive from safety training:

1. **Take it seriously** - remember that your instructor wouldn't be bringing this stuff up unless someone had been injured or killed because of it.
2. **Make connections** - think about how the information relates to your current knowledge and experience. These connections help you retain the information and recall it when you need it most.
3. **Ask questions** - get clarification on important points. Everyone learns better when they understand the "whys" as well as the "whats." This will help energize the other students in the class as well as your instructor.

4. **Offer your own perspective** - be prepared to share personal experiences that can help illustrate the importance of the information. People remember stories told by people they know, especially those that speak of hard safety lessons learned.

5. **Put it to work** - always be thinking about real-world application of your safety knowledge and how you will use it to keep you and your coworkers safe.

The key to getting the most out of your safety training is to be prepared to make your own contribution to the class. Your active participation will inspire others to do the same, making the learning experience that much more worthwhile for everyone. In the end, your efforts to engage with the material will bring you that much closer to attaining your personal safety goals.

—⁘—

Principle #3: A true student of safety takes responsibility for their own learning.

Question to Consider: How much of your safety knowledge has led you to work more safely?

—⁘—

5

Delivering the message

"Courage is what it takes to stand up and speak; courage is also what it takes to sit down and listen."

— WINSTON CHURCHILL

I f you accept the ideas presented in Chapter 3, you agree that you bear responsibility for your coworker's safety. For purposes of review, this is summarized in three presuppositions:

1. No one person can have enough information to always act safely.
2. Each and every one of your coworkers will have a different perspective and can be a source of valuable safety information.

3. Everyone bears responsibility for their coworker's safety. In other words, you are your brother's keeper.

The implications are clear. You have made a commitment to watch out for your fellow employees, and are prepared to intervene if you believe their safety is in question.

Your commitment to the safety of your coworkers could be tested under conditions where there isn't any time for diplomacy. The circumstances could be dire enough that you need to jump in and get someone's attention right away. You may raise your voice and use a tone that you wouldn't ordinarily use, but you're not going to hesitate because something bad is going to happen if you don't. This is a situation where careful consideration is not going to help; you must react immediately to stop someone from getting hurt or killed.

As I described in Chapter 4, I had an experience like this when I was working as an automotive technology instructor. My students were in the lab during an electrical systems class, and I was observing one of them as he demonstrated how to use a battery charger. He had been fast-charging a dead battery, and was preparing to disconnect the charger leads before attempting to start the vehicle. To my dismay, he tried to disconnect the battery charger while it was still turned on, potentially creating sparks that could cause a battery explosion. I shouted STOP! before he pulled the leads off, causing him to let go but leaving him visibly shaken. I immediately apologized to him for my harsh response, but reminded him that he and I both could have been hurt if the vehicle's battery had exploded. There was no time for considering what to do or say; I had to get him stopped *now*. This was a teachable moment, one that he is not likely to forget.

This kind of safety interaction is straightforward, in the sense that you know exactly what you need to do and you aren't worried about hurting people's feelings. However, this is also a relatively rare occurrence. The majority of the times that you are confronted with a safety issue, it doesn't involve obvious danger. In these situations, approaching another person with a safety concern can be a difficult exercise. Things turn out to be more complicated than we expected, and we don't do what we know we should. Why does this happen? There are numerous factors that stop us from sharing safety concerns with our coworkers.

I lack experience. If you are young in years or new to the industry, you may be unsure of yourself and your judgment. This can make you hesitate to bring up safety concerns because you believe that your coworkers know better than you.

I lack authority. Because you are low on your company's totem pole, you've convinced yourself that people won't listen to you - even if you have a valid safety concern.

I'm only a contractor. The safety culture on your worksite may be such that contractors are treated as second-class citizens. The established pecking order may cause contractors to withdraw from safety interactions because they have concluded that company employees will not listen to them.

I'm not sure about the company policy. We often use company policy as our yardstick to determine whether a procedure is safe or not, and you may not recall what the current policy states. Another possibility is that the policy isn't clear on the issue, or hasn't been updated to reflect current practice.

I don't know the person. It's risky on an emotional level when you don't know the person who you need to discuss a safety concern with. You'd like to hope for the best, but what if they don't warm up to what you're saying? Will they ignore you or even get angry with you?

I know the person too well. Sometimes, it is more difficult to bring up safety concerns with someone you know, especially if you've had negative interactions with them in the past. Even with someone you're on good terms with, you may be afraid of embarrassing them and possibly jeopardizing your relationship. You could also look like a hypocrite if it's common knowledge that you don't follow the rules yourself.

I don't want the boss to get angry with me. For the most part, supervisors don't have a problem pointing out safety issues with people that work for them. However, it doesn't always flow the same in the opposite direction. Workers sometimes hesitate to approach their superiors with safety concerns because they fear they could be misunderstood. If your boss views your concerns as insubordination, they may use their power to make your life difficult. In extreme cases, this could lead to retaliatory behavior such as a poor evaluation or even disciplinary action.

I had a bad experience the last time. In a perfect world, we would be able to express safety concerns freely with our fellow employees. Our coworkers would see the value in our observations and always thank us for taking the time to help them stay safe.

Right.

Time for a reality check. How often do safety interactions turn out the way we want them to? All too often, our coworkers are not receptive to our overtures. In fact, if things go really poorly, they may not just ignore your advice, but could also lash out at you. The end result is that we regret bringing up the concern in the first place, and are less likely to do so in the future.

WHAT TO DO
The issue of bringing up safety concerns with our coworkers can be complex. There are many reasons why we hesitate, some of them inspired by our personal insecurities and others related to factors external to ourselves. In order

to move forward, we need a strategy that can simplify safety interactions and make it easier to overcome our reluctance to get involved.

A common reason for your safety concern to be rejected is that the receiver thinks you are attempting to make them look bad. Having said that, your main objective is to convince the receiver that you are on their side. This can be challenging because some folks are more apt to assume the worst about people's intentions.

A simple method for limiting the possibility of a confrontation while addressing a safety concern is to make a statement that communicates that you want to help. To understand why this can be an effective strategy, we need to walk a mile in the shoes of the person at the receiving end.

First off, nobody likes to be embarrassed. If we approach a person with a blunt statement about how they are doing something unsafe, it can appear that we are calling them stupid.

Put on a face shield when you are grinding.
Why don't you have a tag line on that suspended load?
You know better than to use a screwdriver as a pry tool.

Statements like these put your coworkers on the defensive. You may also give them the impression that you are less interested in their safety than in making you look smarter than them. When people become defensive, it generally results in one of two kinds of behavior: fight or flight. They can argue with you and attempt to justify their actions, or they can ignore you altogether and continue doing what they were doing. Neither of these reactions will help anyone achieve their personal safety goals. Consider these alternatives to the previous statements:

> *Can I get you a faceshield?*
> *Let me find a tag line before we make this lift.*
> *I have a pry bar you can use.*

We need to keep in mind that everyone wants to be respected by their peers. If our words or actions serve to diminish another person's feeling of importance, a negative outcome is assured. Even if the person does what you tell them this time, they are more likely to be resistant to your overtures in the future.

ASKING A QUESTION

Asking a well-crafted question can serve to reinforce a person's feeling of importance. This is because you no longer appear to be condemning them, but are instead deferring to their knowledge and judgment on the issue. This approach will immediately disarm the person engaging in risky behavior and encourage them to be more open to what you have to say. You can then address the situation with a higher likelihood of success. As you continue, questions will remain more helpful than blunt statements. Consider how these kinds of questions promote teamwork:

> *What do you think of the way that machine is supported?*
> *What equipment could we use to make this lift easier?*
> *How can we position the work to make our job safer?*

Note the use of the words "we" and "our." This tells the listener that you are an active participant in the process and are working with everyone else as a team to get the job done safely. The solution is no longer "my idea" and is now "your idea" or "our idea." The chances of the safety interaction concluding successfully are that much greater because everyone (including you) has had their confidence and feeling of importance enhanced. Most importantly, we are more likely to work safer when we can achieve this dynamic.

Do you insist that everyone else adopt your idea? Holding tightly to this puts you at a disadvantage when it comes to attaining your personal safety goals. Soliciting the opinions of others and acknowledging the ideas that are better than yours increases people's willingness to work with you. Beyond that, it serves to solidify your leadership position because your coworkers recognize that you are more concerned about being safe than being right.

There is a simple question you can ask that tells others that you are deferring to their judgment and expertise:

How can I help?

When is the last time you heard a coworker utter those words? The recipient of this question will immediately recognize that you are on their side. Once the ice is broken with this initial interaction, they will also be that much more open to your suggestions.

To be clear, there are also wrong ways to ask a question. You can just as easily convey an attitude of arrogance when asking a question as you can by making a blunt statement. Some examples of less-than-optimal questions:

What do you think you're doing?
Didn't anyone show you how to adjust your fall harness?
Where are your safety glasses?

Certainly, your choice of words is most important, but you must also consider the way you deliver your message. Think carefully about the tone of your voice and body language before you approach a coworker with a safety concern. You could have the words right, but still mess things up by speaking to the listener in a condescending tone or making hand gestures that can be interpreted as accusations.

I would suggest that you will overcome many of the pitfalls in safety interactions by playing the role of a student. If you are the student and the person you are approaching is the teacher, much of the potential for conflict goes away. Being a student implies that you have respect for them and that you truly desire to know what they know. You will enhance the other person's feeling of importance as well as learning some things that you didn't know before. You may also discover that the other person becomes more interested in hearing your opinions, and could decide to learn something from you as well.

Maintaining the mindset of a student can help you in other areas of your work life. Asking questions in such a way that the listener feels that you truly want to learn will reinforce professional relationships and help you get your job done better. The bottom line is that you are paying respect to others and this often inspires others to do the same for you.

Doing your best to make other people look good is fundamental to prosperity in your work life, but above all, it will serve to help you achieve your personal safety goals.

WHEN THINGS GO WRONG

You can't win 'em all. There are going to be times when you do everything you can to be diplomatic when offering a safety concern, but the receiver isn't receptive to what you have to say. The receiver could ignore you, tell you to mind your own business, or even heap abuse on you. A possible consequence of a negative response is that you could decide to avoid safety interactions in the future. This dynamic, left unchecked, can serve to jeopardize your safety along with that of everyone you work with.

You cannot allow yourself to be defeated by a negative safety interaction. Clearly, it takes some grit to rebound from such an experience, but it is critical that you not take it personally and continue to press to the goal. Keep in mind that their response may be less about them not liking you than it is about them not liking themselves. Mahatma Gandhi once said "Nobody can hurt me without my permission." The reality is that if your feelings are hurt by a negative response to your safety concern, it is because you choose to be hurt.

It also helps to walk a mile in the receiver's shoes. Maybe they are struggling with personal problems, or it's possible they misunderstood your intentions when you approached them with your concern. Even if this interaction didn't work out, it may turn out different with this person in the future. The benefit of the doubt goes a long way towards building relationships with people who appear to have tough exteriors. Your response could boil down to a simple act of discipline, but it is ultimately a test of your commitment to your personal safety as well as that of your coworkers.

Principle #4: Always offer to help when delivering a safety concern.

Question to Consider: Do you allow your feelings to be hurt when a coworker rejects your attempt to keep them safe?

6

Receiving the message

*"In my walks, every man I meet is my superior
in some way, and in that I learn from him."*

- Ralph Waldo Emerson

Safety interactions are one of the great challenges of the modern workplace. As discussed in Chapter 5, an interaction is initiated by a person with a safety concern. That person, the giver of safety advice, is tasked with the responsibility of delivering the message to the receiver. In a healthy workplace, the receiver is not just willing to listen to the message, but will also take steps to deal with the safety hazard.

Who is at fault if things don't go the way they should? There are two possible ways that a failed safety interaction can play out:

Scenario 1 - the giver delivered the message and the receiver rejected it; or

Scenario 2 - the giver didn't follow through on delivering the message.

Our natural inclination is to blame the giver of safety advice for both of these failures. In Scenario 1, we could conclude that the giver didn't use the right approach, whereas in Scenario 2, the giver of safety advice lacked moral courage. Pretty straightforward.

Not so fast. What is the receiver's responsibility in all this? We are often quick to condemn the actions of the giver, but it is also possible that the receiver is at least partially to blame for a failed safety interaction.

In the case of Scenario 1, there are a number of reasons why the messages delivered by the givers of safety advice could be rejected by the receiver:

I've always done it this way. While it may not be the safest way to do it, the receiver has gotten away with doing it their way enough times that it has become personal standard practice. Their assumption is that since it has always worked in the past, it will continue to work in the future. The mindset of the receiver is to resent anyone who suggests that there could be a safer way of completing the task.

I don't have time to consider a different idea. The receiver has a timeline, and isn't willing to consider a plan that may result in the task taking more time than they budgeted. Pressure to get the job done could be coming from a supervisor, but more likely it is a deadline that the receiver has created in their own mind.

I'm having a bad day. There could be events taking place in the receiver's personal life that are complicating their interactions with coworkers. The issues could be temporary in nature, such as fatigue, or they could be chronic and not likely to go away anytime soon. Certainly, the giver of safety advice may not be aware of these problems when they offer their safety advice, and could take it personally if they receive a negative response.

You aren't qualified to give me safety advice. The receiver of safety advice may hold the giver in low regard due to a perceived lack of experience, knowledge, or credentials. In such a case, the receiver regards the abilities of the giver to be inferior to their own, and is unwilling to consider any suggestions they come up with. This can also be related to factors such as age or gender.

You don't have the authority to give me safety advice. In the receiver's mind, the company hierarchy dictates who listens to whom. The concept of teamwork and looking out for one's coworkers is completely lost on them.

I don't trust you. The receiver doesn't think that the giver has their best interests in mind. They may believe that the giver is trying to embarrass or belittle them, as opposed to achieving best safety practice.

Regarding Scenario 2, why did the giver fail to deliver the message? Yes, they lacked the fortitude to follow through, but what made them decide to not take the risk?

The root cause of the failure to communicate could have everything to do with the receiver's safety image. Your safety image is how others view your attitude and commitment to safety. This is important because your safety image has everything to do with how your coworkers interact with you.

You may not care what other people think of you. However, it pays to consider your safety image in terms of whether people view you as approachable. If you want others to look out for your safety, they need to know that you are open to outside influence.

Playing the role of the giver of safety advice can be risky on an emotional level. For some, it takes all the courage they can gather to approach a coworker with a safety concern. The giver is vulnerable in the sense that they are hoping for the best, but are afraid that the receiver will not be receptive. If the giver of safety advice goes out on a limb and gets rejected, they are less likely to take the risk again. In a corruption of how things ought to be, the giver is being "educated" on what happens to those who look out for their coworkers.

INTROSPECTION

It's time to think about your own mindset. What is your reaction when a coworker approaches you with a safety concern?

Many lack appreciation for how crucial these moments are. A very real "ripple effect" takes place, no matter how you respond. If you are open to the concern and willing to take time to deal with the issue in a collaborative manner, the giver of safety advice is encouraged to continue watching out for your safety. Coworkers that witness your collaborative response are more willing to conduct themselves in a similar fashion, further reinforcing the company's safety culture.

On the other hand, consider the consequences when the giver of safety advice is ignored or ridiculed. The giver mustered the courage to follow through and deliver the message, and now is being beaten with a stick. As the interaction unfolds, the giver makes some mental notes to self, including thinking twice before offering this person safety advice again. More tragic is the fact that they are now less likely to offer anyone safety advice in the future. The dynamic of "once bitten, twice shy" becomes real.

What impact has the failed interaction made on the safety image of the receiver? The receiver is developing the reputation of being someone who isn't interested in hearing other people's safety concerns and may even inflict abuse on anyone that tries. The effect is compounded if the interaction is witnessed by others. Now everyone is withdrawing from the receiver, and won't be available to help when they are needed the most.

I once witnessed a failed interaction where a member of a company's safety department approached a worker about why a safety device was not being used while a machine was being repaired. Because the machine was disassembled extensively, use of the safety device was not necessary and would only serve to hinder the repair operations. However, instead of respectfully explaining the reasoning behind his methods, the technician responded with sarcasm and made the safety person regret approaching him in the first place. A number of other technicians were in the vicinity when this took place, and it grew into a chorus of mockery in the break room shortly thereafter.

This event contributed to the "education" of a number of people. The safety department person learned that this worker was likely to respond negatively when approached with a safety concern, and he would definitely be gun shy if faced with a similar situation in the future. Other workers who witnessed the interaction learned that they too would be ridiculed if they did the same thing. The end result was that everyone involved became more reluctant to assume the role of the giver of safety advice. Sadly, this may lead to an incident that could have been avoided if workers felt "safe" when approaching their coworkers with a safety concern.

THE BENEFIT OF THE DOUBT

The way you respond to a giver of safety advice is mostly determined by what you believe their intentions to be. You can't know for sure what their motivations are when they approach you with a safety concern, so you are left to make an assumption. If you choose to believe that the giver is trying to keep you safe, you are very likely to hear out their concern and therefore stand a good chance of working through the issue in a collaborative manner. This doesn't necessarily mean that you agree with their suggestion, but it does mean you take time to listen and explore its merits. This may also lead to an even better plan that springs out of a newly formed creative collaboration.

The alternative is to adopt the position that the giver of safety advice is trying to embarrass you, get you in trouble, or slow you up. Accordingly, you're not going to take the time to listen because you are "turtling" and you adopt a defensive stance where you block out external voices. In this mode, you will simply ignore the giver and go on with your business, or worse, respond with a stinging rebuke to ensure they never try that again. You're going to get this job done your way, right away.

But what if the giver of safety advice is right?

A fellow I know (I'll call him John) tells the story of an incident that took place many years ago while working at a mining camp in central Alaska. John was young relative to most of the other workers, and was employed by a contractor as a mechanic/welder for the mobile equipment on the mine site.

The company was using diesel-powered scrapers to remove the material that lay on top of the ore-bearing rock. The scrapers needed frequent service, which often required removal of the belly pan located under the engine compartment. The belly pan was made of heavy plate steel, with hinges on one side that would allow it to swing down and to the side when the mounting bolts were removed. The removal procedure had a high potential for injury because the belly pan was extremely heavy and the mechanic was required to work underneath it during the removal process.

The safest way to remove the belly pan was to attach a chain hoist to the frame of the machine, and then run the chain under the pan and connect it to the frame on the opposite side. A block of wood could then be placed between the chain and the pan, after which the chain hoist was tightened. All of the mounting bolts could then be removed at once, and the pan was lowered slowly using the chain hoist. While this method was safer, it took more time because there were multiple steps and more equipment involved.

A mechanic could save time by removing all but one of the bolts with an air wrench, then support the pan with his feet as he lay with his back on the ground. The next step was to reach up with the air wrench and remove the final bolt, and then lower the belly pan with their legs so it could swing down and out of the way. This shortcut worked as long as there wasn't any material piled up on top of the belly pan, which would collect over time and make it dangerously heavy. It also would not work if the belly pan's hinges were broken because the pan would then drop straight down instead of swinging to the side. John was well aware of these hazards, and was thinking about what could go wrong as he observed a company mechanic preparing to lower the belly pan on a disabled scraper.

John took the time to approach the mechanic and let him know that the belly pan may have dirt on top of it and thus be too heavy to use the shortcut method.

John also offered to lend him a chain hoist if that would help. The mechanic, now playing the role of the receiver, immediately rejected John's suggestion and uttered an expletive that strongly suggested that he mind his own business.

John backed off from the confrontation and returned to his service truck to continue with his own work. Shortly thereafter, he heard a scream come from the direction of the disabled scraper. John ran to help, and as he approached he could see that the mechanic was lying underneath with the belly pan on top of him. It was obvious that the belly pan had indeed collected a massive amount of dirt on top of it, making it impossible for the mechanic to hold it up with his legs. Beyond that, the hinges were broken and when the mechanic removed the last bolt with his air wrench, the entire assembly came down on top of him. The mechanic's legs were crushed under the tremendous load, and he continued to scream as his coworkers tried to retrieve him from underneath the machine.

This incident became only more tragic as time went on, as the mechanic never recovered and within six months had died of complications related to his injuries.

What was the mechanic thinking when John offered him his safety advice? There's no way of knowing for sure, but here are a few possibilities:

Your way is going to take too much time.
You aren't my boss.
I've been doing this a lot longer than you have.
You must think I am stupid.
You are trying to make me look bad.

Clearly, the mechanic chose to assume the worst. Things would have played out very differently had he given John the benefit of the doubt.

The kid took the time to walk over here and warn me about this situation. I better take the time to hear him out.

Let's be clear on this…you are in command of your assumptions. If you choose to believe the worst about someone who is trying to give you safety advice, you are that much closer to jeopardizing your safety as well as that of your coworkers. Choosing to grant the messenger the benefit of the doubt will give you the best chance of achieving your personal safety goals.

———⚏———

Principle #5: The benefit of the doubt will lead you to a safer solution *every time*.

Question to Consider: How do you respond to a coworker who shares a safety concern?

———⚏———

7

Enhancing your safety image

"There is only one corner of the universe you can be certain of improving, and that's your own self."

- ALDOUS HUXLEY

A healthy workplace will demonstrate a spirit of collegiality. Collegiality is the mutual respect and shared responsibility among colleagues united in a common purpose. It implies trust among coworkers, as all work towards building a safe and productive workplace.

Unfortunately, it is common for workplaces to be something less than collegial. This creates complications for the worker who intends to practice safety and do all they can to keep their coworkers safe. If you are not in a leadership position, what can you do to influence your company's safety culture for the better?

First off, you cannot let apathy and nonaction of your co-workers discourage you from pursuing your personal safety goals. Nothing is more important than staying safe. There are people that count on you to come home safely every day. You owe it to yourself and the others in your life to work safely.

You must also keep in mind that the only person you can change is yourself. In other words, it starts with you. There is no point in getting frustrated about the people around you; start with a plan on how to improve yourself and set an example for others to follow. This begins with a self-evaluation of your safety image.

The concept of safety image is pivotal in regards to attaining your personal safety goals. Remember the definition of safety image from Chapter 6? It describes how your coworkers view your attitude and commitment to safety. Your safety image can serve to encourage your coworkers, motivating them to work together to be safe. However, it can just as easily be a negative influence, putting a damper on collaboration and safe behaviors.

When a coworker is trying to decide whether to approach you with a safety concern, your safety image will have everything to do with whether they follow through. Your safety image helps answer the following questions for the giver of safety advice:

1. Is this person open to outside influence?
2. How will I be treated if I approach this person with a safety concern?

If you are viewed as being closed minded and possibly hostile towards those who give you safety advice, your coworkers are not likely to share their concerns. You could even fool yourself into thinking that because nobody ever gives you safety advice, you must be a safe worker. There will come a time that you need your coworkers to keep an eye out for you, and they may not be there. Clearly, it pays for each of us to consider our safety image and whether it is helping us attain our personal safety goals.

The business of seeing yourself through the eyes of your coworkers can be a challenging and even painful exercise. Do you really want to know what people think of you? If you have doubts, you may be on to something. Without going any further, you've probably already determined that your safety image could benefit from a tune-up. In this chapter, we will discuss practical ways to enhance your safety image, which will also benefit your coworkers and reinforce the safety culture of your company.

ASK QUESTIONS

Many of us attend safety meetings on a regular basis; in some cases, more than one per day. After a while, you start to hear the same topics over and over again and you may decide to "tune out." Safety meetings are sometimes held in the same contempt as getting a needle; it has to be done, let's just get it over with. This kind of attitude has a negative effect on your safety image, and can lead your coworkers to conclude that safety is not your gig.

The subject of disengagement from the learning process was discussed in Chapter 4 of this book. Many man-hours are spent sitting through safety training and safety meetings, but how much of it turns into changed behavior on the part of the attendees? For those who have withdrawn from the discussion, the net effect is almost nil. The tragic side of this is that they could be utilizing the time to make gains in their personal growth, and could also be making a contribution to others in the group.

A true student of safety takes responsibility for their own learning, and disciplines themselves to actively engage in safety discussions. One of the most effective ways to do this is to ask good questions. There are some compelling reasons why this strategy will help you and your coworkers.

Clarification. Nobody wants to feel as though they are the only one that doesn't understand. This is why many workers don't ask questions during safety training, even when they decide the information could be useful to them. I have been in more than one class where I asked a question, then had other students approach me afterwards to say they were really glad I asked because they didn't understand either. This takes some maturity on your part... you have to get over caring whether someone thinks you are a slow learner. From my experience, most people are glad that you went ahead and asked the question and they respect your courage for doing so. This strategy will enhance your safety image because your coworkers will realize that you care enough about safety to risk looking dumb. A side benefit is that it will encourage your coworkers to ask questions as well.

Feedback to the instructor. A good safety instructor will figure out ways to get workers to engage no matter what their personality type, and will always be looking for signs that they are comprehending the material. Not all instructors will do that (for various reasons), so workers that are willing to ask questions can help extract maximum value out of the time spent in the class. In some cases, the instructor may believe that their teaching ability is more effective than it really is. Asking questions during class can help the instructor see more clearly where they need to work on their delivery, and can also energize them because they can see that the workers really want to learn.

SHARE STORIES

One of the most powerful strategies you can use to persuade an audience is to illustrate your point with a story that they can relate to. Simply stating an idea has limited effect; a whole new understanding can be achieved when the information is reinforced by an anecdote or analogy that shows why it is true. This technique is used by writers, teachers, preachers and politicians, and can be utilized effectively for enhancing safety discussions.

All people, regardless of race or culture, remember stories. This is the foundation of oral tradition; humans have used this method to pass down values and beliefs to their children since the beginning of time. Stories bring a new level of relevance to the topic at hand, and make it that much easier for the listener to remember the point and then share it with others. One reason that stories are so effective for teaching is because they stir emotions, which play a vital role in the human learning process. Without emotions being engaged, new information doesn't get traction in the listener's mind and isn't given the opportunity to change behavior.

A former mine superintendent related a story to me regarding a fatality that took place at an underground mine he worked at years ago. After he started to tell the story, he paused and asked for my patience because he knew he was going to get emotional. A miner that worked for him had died while loading hauling units, a death that was caused by a bad decision on the part of the miner. It was a difficult story to tell because it was so close to his heart. Regardless of whose fault it was, it had happened on his watch and he wasn't ever going to forget.

While I didn't know the superintendent very well at that time, I gained a greater appreciation for his courage and commitment to safety when he told me his story. He wasn't the only one that got emotional; I was relating to his sense of loss and remorse for what happened. As painful as it was, he was using his experience to help others sort through their priorities when making safety decisions.

What made the superintendent's story so powerful was that it was his own. Think about this for a moment. You're going to be much more passionate telling about your own experiences than you will be about someone else's. Your passion grabs the attention of the listener and inspires them to engage with the topic at hand. You could say that you've been "promoted" because you can speak with authority on that issue and your coworkers are more likely to listen. All of this works together to enhance your safety image because your coworkers can relate to you better and you become more approachable in their eyes.

Hearing someone else's safety story will sometimes lead you to make connections with experiences from your past. This can give you a new perspective on the other person's story as well as your own. Engagement at this level is an example of deep learning, a process that has an excellent chance of changing behaviors. These are teachable moments; you should be ready to share your reflections with your coworkers when the opportunity arises.

If you are hesitating to share your story because you are afraid of speaking in public, you need to keep one thing in mind. The audience is just as embarrassed as you if you fail in the delivery of your story. In other words, your audience wants you to be successful. Speak with confidence because they are on your side.

At a minimum, be sure to thank the person who shared their safety story, and encourage them to share more stories in the future. For some, the act of speaking in public could take all of the courage they can muster, so kind words from their coworkers can go a long way toward boosting their confidence and help them make similar contributions down the road.

TEACH WHAT YOU LEARN

Teaching safety to others will often take place in informal settings during the regular work day. It could happen during a safety interaction, where a coworker has a question or you initiate a conversation with someone who needs assistance in their safety practice. These interactions are growth opportunities regardless of whether you play the role of the teacher or the student. In a perfect world, these roles are interchangeable...the teacher can learn just as much as the student - if they have the right mindset.

The best way to learn a subject thoroughly is to teach it to someone else. It is easy to fool ourselves into believing that we know a subject well. However, gaps in our knowledge are exposed quickly when we attempt to communicate it to another person.

This is a fundamental principle behind the Montessori Method of education. Students that have mastered a lesson are tasked with teaching that same material to younger children. The opportunity for growth with this model is immense because the students doing the teaching are improving their communication skills while they reinforce the information they just learned. Questions from the younger students serve to illuminate areas where they need more information, and the challenge of teaching another person stirs their creativity.

One of the reasons for the success of the Montessori Method is because it establishes a strong "need to know" in the mind of the teacher. Adults, in particular, need good reasons to put time and energy into learning something. In other words, they need to understand that there will be a tangible benefit for putting forth the effort. Teaching someone a skill or information you just learned gives you a need to know because you don't want to appear misinformed or incompetent to your students; you will work hard to avoid that kind of embarrassment. If you suddenly get a question that you can't answer, you will often do what it takes to get an answer and relay it to the person who asked the question. That information has now gained importance in the mind of the teacher, and they aren't likely to forget it. Good teachers learn just as much, if not more than their students.

In the same manner, your students will learn better if they have a need to know what you are teaching. The teacher's job becomes that much easier when they can give the student a reason to want to know the information. Fortunately, this isn't difficult when teaching safety because there is a direct practical application for the information.

Keep in mind that it is possible to tarnish your safety image while teaching safety. Being opinionated and inflexible gives others the impression that you aren't interested in what they have to say. This can lead your students to conclude that you don't want them to offer you safety concerns. Maintaining an air of humility is critical for a teacher; you need to let people know that you are a student as well, and that you are open to correction.

I have a friend who is considered to be one of the top automotive trainers in the country. He presents seminars at conferences all over the U.S. and is a subject matter expert at the level where "when he talks, everybody listens." Despite his widely acknowledged expertise, he has not let it go to his head. He will seek out opinions and thoughts from his audience, and will acknowledge information that he was not aware of. On more than one occasion, I have heard him say "I hadn't thought of that" in response to a comment from a student. His image is one of humility and teachability, which serves to inspire his students to do the same. This is the kind of approach we can all learn from, which is maintaining confidence in our own abilities while understanding there is still a great deal that we don't know.

ENCOURAGE OTHERS

We don't give enough credit to those who offer us safety advice. Many people have to summon all the courage they can to get past the natural inhibitions that prevent them from bringing up safety concerns with their coworkers. When we appreciate the grit it takes for a coworker to follow through on this, we see that person in a new light. These are crucial moments; they cared enough to take a risk and express their concern, and now you need to acknowledge their contribution.

Heartfelt "thank yous" are a precious commodity in the workplace. Keep in mind that even if your coworker was misinformed, you still need to thank them for taking the time to offer their concern. Some people may be afraid of encouraging their coworkers to speak up because they think it could turn into this person constantly intervening in their work. It's time to go beyond this type of thinking. We all need to be working on ideas on how to encourage our coworkers to approach us when they have safety concerns. To do otherwise is not an option.

At the same time, we should also be aware of how our personal safety decisions can serve to discourage our coworkers from offering their safety concerns. Specifically, we are talking about "practicing what we preach." If you tell others about safety rules and the correct way of going about things, and then do the opposite, you undermine your safety image. Your coworkers will conclude that you are a hypocrite and that this safety stuff is not as important as you made it out to be. This can lead your coworkers to withdraw from interactions with you, as well as with others.

You have much greater influence than you realize. Things you do and say to enhance your safety image will make a contribution to the safety of your coworkers as well as the safety culture of your company.

Principle #6: Your personal safety goals become more achievable when you contribute to the safety of others.

Question to Consider: What are some ways that you can encourage your coworkers to approach you with safety concerns?

8

A self-imposed sense of urgency

"The two most powerful warriors are patience and time."

- LEO TOLSTOY

A common utterance in the world of business is "time is money." The idea behind the saying is that taking more time on a project generally results in more money being spent. While the basic principle is true, it is also understood that there is a point of diminishing returns on getting a job done faster. In other words, you can only work so fast and continue to save money; you eventually reach a point where going faster will only increase your costs.

One aspect of a project that suffers with increased haste is quality. The faster you go, the more difficult it is to turn out good work. This can increase costs when the customer demands that you do it over. Over the long-term, shoddy craftsmanship could harm your reputation and make it difficult to find more work.

There is also a point where going faster begins to jeopardize worker safety. To save time, workers sometimes choose to take risks that can result in injuries. The industrial world has seen more than its fair share of incidents that took place because saving time was considered to be more important than worker safety. In many cases, we get away with it and nothing bad happens despite the increased risks. These "successes" often serve to embolden us and make it easier to assume increased risks in the future. There always comes a time, however, when the "winning streak" is over and an incident is the end result.

An example of "haste makes waste" from the construction world is a catastrophic incident that took place during the construction of Miller Park baseball stadium in Milwaukee, Wisconsin. The contractor that was responsible for construction of the stadium's retractable roof had already installed several major pieces and was preparing to place the next section. Per the contract, finishing ahead of time and under budget would result in a bonus being paid out. However, the contractor was under tremendous pressure because the project was behind schedule and over budget, and financial penalties would be assessed if that trend continued.

On the late afternoon of July 14, 1999, a massive crane known as Big Blue was waiting to lift the next 450-ton section of Miller Park's roof. Conditions were sunny and warm but windy that day, with gusts of up to 27 miles per hour. This was problematic for the contractor because the crane manufacturer specified that Big Blue should not be operated in winds higher than 20 miles per hour. Another factor that may have been underestimated was the lattice design of the massive roof section, which generated significant wind resistance and could serve to further decrease the stability of the crane.

The crane crew had been on standby all that day, waiting for conditions to change. Despite the wind speeds that afternoon, the contractor decided to push forward with the work. Big Blue got underway, lifting the roof section high over the stadium and then slowly lowering it into position. Three ironworkers who were to fasten the roof section into place awaited in a man basket that was suspended from a crane located inside the stadium.

A video of the incident taken from the ground level tells the remainder of the story in graphic detail. As the roof section is slowly being lowered, a screeching noise is heard followed by two loud bangs. The crane slowly keels over, and the main boom folds up as it falls over top of the stadium walls. The roof section falls inside the stadium, taking the three ironworkers to their deaths as they fell nearly 300 feet to the ground level. By the time the dust settles, the Miller Park roof project is a mass of twisted metal lying on the stadium seats and floor.

The emotional and financial costs of this catastrophe are immense. Subsequent to the incident investigation and a prolonged trial, a jury awarded $97 million in civil and punitive damages to the widows of the three ironworkers. Miller Park's initial construction cost was estimated at $322 million. However, stadium completion was delayed by an entire year, with the final bill coming in at $414 million. This figure did not include $100 million in repair costs that was covered by insurance, or the millions of dollars in additional interest paid by Milwaukee taxpayers on the bonds that were sold to pay for the stadium.[3]

Would it have been worth it for the contractor to wait for a day that wasn't so windy? Based on what we know now, the answer is an emphatic yes. In the heat of the moment, however, it didn't seem so clear. This incident is an illustration of how easy it is to let schedules dictate our actions, no matter what risks we assume in the process. It also tells us what the costs can be when we push too hard to get a difficult task done right away. The Big Blue crane incident is now a case study that illustrates how much cheaper it can be to take the time to do it right.

ON A PERSONAL NOTE

It's easy for us to dismiss the Big Blue incident as the kind of thing that happens with greedy company owners, but doesn't apply to us on the ground level. The fact is that the same dynamic plays out regularly in us as individuals. Unfortunately, most workers are unaware of this and how their own thinking can work against them in regards to achieving their personal safety goals.

A simple example of this is the number of times we are hurrying to get something done, and on the way we notice an unsafe condition that needs to be addressed. Is your automatic response to stop and make sure that the safety concern is dealt with appropriately? Naturally, this will take time and you had it in mind that you wanted to get this other task completed as soon as possible. Our default is often to continue on our way and tell ourselves that we will circle back to the safety concern later. Without thinking it in so many words, we are affirming that saving time is more important than safety.

This dynamic plays out far more often than we realize. Every day, we are faced with performing tasks and many of these have some level of urgency attached to them. Where is the pressure coming from to get these tasks done right away? Take some time to think about this. You may surprise yourself when you realize that often the expectation to get a task done immediately is mostly pressure you are putting on yourself. This is known as a *self-imposed sense of urgency*.

This is not to say that your supervisor doesn't care how long it takes to get the job done. Certainly, from their perspective, faster is better. However, if working faster means the possibility of damaging equipment or getting someone hurt, your supervisor should be willing to adjust their timeline accordingly.

The people performing the task are often less flexible with their timelines. Some possible reasons for this include:

1. We want to please our supervisor.
2. We don't want to look bad in front of our coworkers.
3. We have a personal time limit for completing the task.

We all want to please our supervisor. This even applies to supervisors we don't like. We would much rather get a task completed and make our supervisor happy with our performance than have to report to them that a task is going to take longer than anticipated. This could be inspired by fear because your supervisor has a certain level of control over how things go for you at work. The fear could be that you will be put on the supervisor's "black list" if you don't get your work done in a timely manner. They could write you a poor evaluation, deny you a promotion or pay upgrade, or start giving you less than desirable job assignments. You may also be afraid of being laid off or fired.

However, the reverse could be true. It could be that you have a good relationship with your supervisor and are working hard to do your best for them. In an effort to make them look good, you tend to push to get things done promptly. These good intentions can also influence your decision making for the worse. A job isn't going well and you decide to take inappropriate risks to get it done right away and keep your supervisor out of hot water.

Sometimes, the issue is rooted in our own insecurity. We may be sensitive to how our coworkers view us and our capabilities. Making the call to slow the job down could be viewed as incompetence or a lack of courage. Or it could cause an inconvenience for your coworkers, making you the focus of their ire. To coin a contemporary phrase, you don't want to be "that guy." To avoid these negative outcomes, you may tend to take risks in an effort to get your jobs done on time and keep the spotlight off yourself.

If this describes you, it's time to ask yourself some tough questions. Are you placing a higher priority on your public image than on the safety of yourself and your coworkers? How is your mindset serving to help you reach your personal safety goals?

It is possible that the most common cause for a self-imposed sense of urgency is the time limits you've established for yourself to complete the job. As you prepare to get underway, you may not be aware that you have already estimated how much time it should take to get the job done. Early in the game, your mind is already working against you as it sets up limitations and an associated inflexibility in your thinking.

Things get more complicated if you expect to be done by the time that another scheduled event is to take place that day, such as a meeting or the end of the work day. You've put yourself in a difficult situation because your mind is set on finishing up by a certain time. Anything that goes wrong with the job will only serve to frustrate you and could tempt you to decide to take shortcuts to meet your self-imposed deadline.

When I was an apprentice heavy duty mechanic, I worked at a truck dealership located on a major highway in Manitoba, Canada. There were four mechanics that worked in the shop, including me and three journeymen. We had many local customers that brought us their trucks for repair, but we also got a lot of "drop in" traffic from long-distance truckers that came in off the highway.

We mechanics in the shop all took a great deal of pride in our work, and we tended to take it personally when jobs didn't come out the way we wanted. Despite the fact that we were all being paid by the hour, we put a lot of pressure on ourselves to get work done in a timely manner. We all had a pretty good idea of how much time each job should take, and we always worked to try to get the work done in that time frame.

It is a good thing to take pride in your work. However, we were a headstrong bunch and didn't adjust very well when things weren't going as we wanted them to. It seemed as though there were always things that stood in the way of getting the job done: no parts, wrong parts, components that were seized together and didn't want to come apart, etc. We had developed a culture where we would let out a well-rehearsed verbal reaction (not to be repeated) when we ran into difficulties, which was sometimes accompanied by a wrench thrown across the shop. Our frustration was also a factor in our decision to do unsafe things at times, when we were struggling to meet the deadline we had established in our mind.

Why were we so tough on ourselves? It had everything to do with unreasonably high expectations and inflexible thinking. Some years later, I had a conversation with one of the mechanics that I worked with at the time. We were talking about how hard we used to push ourselves and our reaction when things didn't go just right. He attributed it to immaturity on our part; there was often little that could be done about the circumstances that frustrated us, and our standard response was not much more than wasted energy. The jobs always got done, but if they took longer it was mostly due to factors outside of our control. Our problem was that we viewed these challenges as a condemnation of our abilities, as opposed to the natural flow of the work process.

This effect may be more pronounced with new employees. When you are new to a job, you tend to be uncertain about the expectations your supervisor has for you and how you are going to fit into this unfamiliar work environment. This can affect your decision making concerning safety because you want to establish right away that you are a productive employee and that they hired the right guy for the job. This can lead a new employee to decide to take inappropriate risks to get the job done.

This is exactly how I felt when I got my first mechanic job. I knew that I was the least experienced guy in the shop, and, in turn, I felt as though I was the most expendable. As a result, I tended to try too hard on some of the jobs I was given, all in an effort to avoid unemployment. An example of this was a day when I was given the job of diagnosing a noise that was coming from the rear end of a school bus. Rather than taking the bus for a test drive first to verify the customer concern, I blazed forward and removed the rear differential assembly from the axle housing. With the differential on the floor, an inspection revealed that there was nothing wrong with it and I had guessed wrong. The differential would have to be reinstalled in the bus, however, it was now late in the afternoon and the hydraulic jack I had used to remove it was tied up in another job. Stinging from my mistake, I steeled my will to have the bus put back together by the end of the work day.

I proceeded to make the decision that it was more important to get the bus reassembled than to wait for the hydraulic jack to become available. A key point here is that I didn't ask anyone else for their thoughts on what I was about to do. Ignoring all fear and common sense, I assumed a crouching position under the bus and lifted the 100-pound differential assembly into place by hand. I was left trembling with adrenaline and exhaustion, but I had accomplished my goal. Although I hadn't determined the cause of the noise, at least the bus was back together.

It is a miracle that I didn't get a hernia or injure my back with this risky maneuver. Upon reflection, it is clear to me that it was one of the stupidest things I have ever done. What was I thinking? Yes, the boss may have been upset if the bus was still in pieces at the end of the day, but was avoiding his displeasure worth the possibility of getting myself hurt? Without hesitation, I can say that the answer is no.

This story is just another example of a worker making bad decisions due to a self-imposed sense of urgency. And, in many cases, the worker isn't as fortunate as I was and ends up suffering an injury that affects them for a lifetime.

RED FLAGS

How does a worker avoid the pitfalls of a self-imposed sense of urgency? The key is being able to think clearly enough at the moment to recognize it for what it is. This can be a test of your maturity because we all tend to get emotional when we are working against a deadline.

A "red flag" that could be telling you to slow down is if you hear yourself thinking,

I could get this done in a few minutes if I just…

This statement is very revealing because it tells you that you have a time limit (quite likely your own) for completing the task. It also indicates that you are about to do something risky, and you are justifying your decision by telling yourself that the possibility of getting the job done right away is worth that risk.

Another indicator of your willingness to take risks is if you look around first to see if anyone is watching. You know what the safety rules are, but you'll intentionally break them if you think you won't get caught.

If you find yourself in one of these situations, you need to stop and step back from the task at hand, then do the following:

1. Take a break, relax, and think about something else for a few minutes.
2. Once you've cleared your head, take a moment to think more carefully about the job and the potential for injury if you push too hard.
3. Fill out a Job Hazard Analysis (JHA) or Job Safety Analysis (JSA) form in cooperation with your co-workers. This will help you assess the risks more

objectively and make a solid plan for doing the job safely.

4. If you can't see a good way to complete the job safely, back off and get your supervisor involved.

A self-imposed sense of urgency is one of the most common hazards in the workplace. Take some time to reflect on whether this plays a role in your safety decision making. Talk about it with your colleagues and put together a plan for how to prevent deadlines from dictating the safety of you and the people you work with.

Principle #7: Deadlines are important, but not more important than safety.

Question to Consider: Is the pressure to get the job done coming from your supervisor, or yourself?

9

Hierarchies

"If your actions inspire others to dream more, learn more, do more and become more, you are a leader."

- JOHN QUINCY ADAMS

We, as humans, spend quite a lot of time figuring out where we sit on the totem pole of life. It seems as though we have a difficult time being happy with who we are. Instead, we tend to use up a lot of energy calculating our personal power ranking. Beyond that, we want to know how we rate when compared to those around us, including our family, our friends, and our coworkers. Measures that we commonly use to assess our position in society include:

1. Money
2. Possessions (house, car, etc.)
3. Education
4. Job title

Our interactions with others are heavily influenced by where we are located in the hierarchies we create in our minds. To be precise, it is our relative ranking that carries the most weight. If we believe that the person we are comparing ourselves to is close to our level, it is easier to relax and build a friendship with that person. However, we tend to act differently with those that we perceive to be at a level other than our own.

Safety interactions can be impacted by this dynamic. Certainly, we have the least difficulty approaching those below us with a safety concern. In our own minds, we have the weight of authority behind us, so it isn't a stretch to ask the less powerful to adjust their behavior. What can they do to us if our overtures aren't appreciated? Not much, and thus we don't view them as a threat. We may also feel as though we don't have to be as careful with our delivery because we hold most of the cards in this scenario.

Coworkers that we consider to be near our level typically receive different treatment. This group is often made up of your peers, which may include people that you don't want to offend. As such, we tend to think more carefully about how we approach them with a safety concern. Our fear could be that this person may withdraw their friendship if we come off as arrogant or obnoxious. Beyond that, your reputation with others in your peer group could also take a turn for the worse. These are typically the people that you spend the most time with during the work day, so keeping the peace with them is a higher priority.

LOOKING UP THE LADDER

The real challenge comes with those who we decide are above us in our hierarchy. The person could be on a higher level on the company organizational chart, or may have more experience than we do. In our minds, these are the people holding the power and that power could be used against us. What could happen if you were to offend this person? For the most part, we aren't worried about their friendship, but what else could they do to us if they didn't appreciate our attempt to help them stay safe?

Our reluctance to address safety concerns with our supervisors isn't always inspired by negative experiences. Many of us were taught from an early age not to talk back to our elders and to always offer them a full measure of respect. These are values that we try to pass on to our children. As our children mature and graduate from school to work, we fully expect that they will give that same respect to their supervisors.

A scene from Frank Capra's 1946 movie classic, *It's a Wonderful Life*, portrays a middle-school aged George Bailey working at a pharmacy owned by Mr. Gower. A horrible mistake had been made by Mr. Gower, where he added poison to a prescription that George was supposed to deliver to a customer. George realized what had happened when he saw the bottle of poison on the counter where the prescription was prepared. However, he couldn't make himself confront his supervisor and, instead, carries the prescription around town for an hour while trying to think of what he should do.

Eventually, George returns to the pharmacy where an angry and abusive Mr. Gower wanted to know why the prescription had not been delivered. Finally, young George blurts out the reason why he hadn't made the delivery. Mr. Gower checked the prescription that George had brought back and knew immediately that he was right. While Gower reversed his course and thanked him for doing the right thing, George was left crying and shaking with fear. George had been raised well and respected his supervisor. Unfortunately, he thought respect meant that you should never say anything to your supervisor that would indicate they had made a mistake.

Certainly, showing respect for your supervisor is a good thing. The problem comes when we equate keeping them safe with disrespect. If you are afraid of speaking up when your supervisor is in peril because you don't want to appear disrespectful, it is time to rethink your position. Just like your coworkers, your supervisor needs you to be willing to say something if their safety is in question.

NEGATIVE INTERACTIONS

My sense is that it is more common for workers to fear their supervisors. This learned behavior is often deep-seated and was probably instilled at a young age. It may have started in the home, or even in school, but negative interactions with our superiors tend to leave a mark.

When I was in high school, the British rock group Pink Floyd was getting a lot of airplay. Their double album, *The Wall*, was released in November 1979, which was during my senior year. *The Wall* is a collection of 26 tracks, including the only number one hit the band ever recorded, *Another Brick in the Wall (Part 2)*[4].

While *Another Brick in the Wall* was Pink Floyd's biggest commercial hit, it was also one of the most controversial. The composer and lyricist, Roger Waters, based the song on his experiences while he was a boarding school student in the UK. In the song, Waters speaks of intellectual and emotional mistreatment at the hands of his teachers, which leads him to call for radical reform of the education system.

At first glance, the cynicism of *Another Brick in the Wall* seems exaggerated. However, it resonated with enough listeners to make it a major hit on music charts around the world. People everywhere related to the song, which may help explain some of the suspicion we harbor for the supervisors in our hierarchies.

The phrase "no good deed goes unpunished" is often used in jest, but the fact that we say it at all is telling. Many workers sense not just a lack of appreciation from those above them, but sometimes veiled hostility. I once heard a maintenance foreman share a story about this very issue at a job site he had worked at. His crew had been in the process of removing a large pump from the bottom of a well on the site. Once the pump was out, the well was open and represented a serious fall hazard. His crew took the time to set up barriers and warning signs around the open hole to keep people away from the area.

At this point in his story, the foreman looked around the room and stated that he had to be careful in case a particular person was present. Lowering his voice, he went on to say that after the barriers were in place around the well, a manager from his company came on the scene to inspect the work. Every other worker on the site stood aghast while the manager proceeded to step over the barriers and stand unrestrained at the edge of the well. The workers were so shocked that they couldn't respond at first, and after a short pause, the foreman composed himself and shouted at the manager to get on the other side of the barrier. By his own description, the words he used lacked civility and were only chosen because of the urgency of the situation.

The manager suddenly awoke to the danger he was in and hurried to get himself to the safe side of the barrier. The foreman had potentially saved his life. Despite that, the interaction left the foreman wondering about what consequences he would face for calling out someone with higher authority than himself. His fear was that he had publicly embarrassed the man and that it would not be forgotten.

All appearances are that the foreman had done the manager a huge favor. If anything, the manager owes him a debt of gratitude. However, despite his willingness to speak up and potentially save his life, the foreman was still afraid that the manager may try to exact revenge on him. Why would he feel this way?

The manager was probably so embarrassed by his mistake that he would rather pretend that it had never happened. While he may not have intended to retaliate, his silence after the fact made the foreman wonder if that wasn't still a possibility. At a minimum, the manager should have openly admitted his mistake and taken the time to thank the foreman for his act of courage. It wasn't just taking the initiative to point out the danger, it was the grit he demonstrated by speaking up despite his natural inhibitions. Unfortunately, a consequence of this incident is that it likely served to increase the foreman's reluctance to speak up the next time he sees a supervisor in peril.

A NOTE TO SUPERVISORS

Being a supervisor isn't for the faint of heart. The job is a tough one at best, and can be complicated by the baggage carried by the folks that work for you. Getting past suspicion and negativity is a daunting task. However, the battle can be won with patience and perseverance.

Demonstrating leadership in safety is a good place to start to gain the trust of your workforce. What you want is to eliminate the inhibitions that prevent your people from approaching you with safety concerns. Like any other worker, you need the people around you to look out for your safety. It starts by admitting you are human. You will make mistakes, and some of those mistakes could jeopardize your and/or someone else's safety. Attempting to maintain an air of invincibility is akin to fighting a war of attrition: nobody wins and both sides get decimated in the end.

You may view this as a risky approach. Won't your workers consider you to be weak if you say out loud that you make mistakes? Your fear could be that you won't be able to motivate them and that you will be taken advantage of if you give up that card. Yes, there are risks involved, but the rewards can be compelling because people respect the courage it takes to admit you are human. Everybody knew it anyway! Beyond that, odds are good that they will do their best to help you succeed when you ask for their help.

The way I see it, you don't have a choice in the matter. Trying to make your workers think you don't make mistakes is basically telling them you won't ever need their help to keep you safe. If you think this way, you and your workers are all in serious trouble.

A manager I know tells the story about a day when he was visiting in his company's equipment repair shop. The shop was a PPE-required area, so at a minimum everyone had to wear a hard hat, steel-toe boots, and safety glasses. Since he wears eye glasses, the manager admits he has a difficult time remembering to put on safety glasses when he goes into the shop. On this particular day, he was talking with the employees in the shop, oblivious to the fact that he didn't have his safety glasses on.

The other workers either didn't notice or were fearful and decided not to say anything. However, one of the shop laborers approached him and stated bluntly, "Aren't you

supposed to be wearing safety glasses like the rest of us?"
The manager says that he felt the hair rise up on the back of
his neck while he processed the safety concern presented to
him by the young employee. His gut reaction was to take
the laborer down a notch using a sharply worded verbal response. However, he stopped himself in time as he realized
the consequences of using that tactic.

Certainly, the laborer's question could have been more
polished. His abruptness came off as though he lacked
respect and didn't care if he embarrassed the manager.
Despite that, there was no denying that he had a legitimate
safety concern. But think about the message that would
have been sent out if the manager had followed through on
his initial reaction.

Imagine yourself as one of the workers in this situation.
What would be your take away if you witnessed the manager chewing out the laborer for speaking up? You and the
other workers in the shop would all make a "note to self"
to not bring up safety concerns with a supervisor again. It
would be natural to conclude that you would suffer the
same consequences if you went down that road.

This story has a great ending. The manager sucked up his pride, thanked the laborer for helping him stay safe, and donned some safety glasses. Fortunately, he was able to assess the potential for damage to the department's safety culture, and then opted to do the right thing. The laborer and the other workers in the shop witnessed an example of safety leadership that day, which reinforced the practice of looking out for others no matter where they stand on the company hierarchy.

LEVEL THE PLAYING FIELD

No matter where you see yourself on the company ladder, you need all others to be looking out for your safety. Everything you do and say around your coworkers should communicate that you need their help, and in turn, you will be doing everything you can to keep them safe. I encourage you to say this in so many words to the people you work with. Let them know that you need them and that their help is much appreciated.

Taking responsibility for your actions is one of the fundamental principles of the safe workplace. If you make a mistake, own it. Doing so will inspire others to follow your lead.

Finally, take some time to think about what stops you from bringing safety concerns to the people you work with, then talk with them about strategies for overcoming those inhibitions. You and your coworkers will all work safer as a result.

—∽—

Principle #8: Safety has no hierarchy.

Question to Consider: What stops you from offering safety concerns to your supervisor?

—∽—

10

Combating complacency

"Success is a lousy teacher. It seduces smart people into thinking they can't lose."

- BILL GATES

The brain is the most complex organ in the human body. Humble in appearance, the human brain is a gelatinous mass made up of 3 pounds of fat and protein. Looks can be deceiving, however, because the brain is the command center for the central nervous system. It is composed of 100 billion nerve cells, which communicate via electrochemical signals on a network made up of trillions of nerve fibers. The brain makes it possible for humans to reason, create art, and make moral judgments. Brain activity also sets the tone for our personalities, as well as involuntary processes such as breathing and digestion.

One of the most amazing functions of the human brain is adaptability. As our brains are exposed to new stimuli, our thought processes change in light of that information. That said, our brains are in a continuous cycle of learning, unlearning, and relearning as we adjust to our evolving environments. This attribute serves us well in our lives, as the conditions we live in rarely stay the same. Some of these changes are within our control, but a great many of them are not. Either way, our brains are constantly acquiring a "new normal," which is our way of making peace with the ever-changing world we live in.

While the human brain demonstrates incredible ability to adapt, it also has a dimension of inflexibility that must be acknowledged. The severity of this effect may vary by individual, but we all tend to be slow to adjust in areas of our lives that remain stable for long periods of time. There is no shortage of real-life examples of this behavior, but one excellent illustration is sudden changes in road conditions that drivers don't adjust to in a timely fashion.

I have lived in Alaska for over 25 years, and my experience has been that winter driving conditions here rarely stay the same for long periods of time. However, a recent winter was unusual because there was very little snow and the roads had been mostly dry and clear for three months. I and two coworkers had flown in to Anchorage on a business trip in early March of that year, and the roads had remained clear up until the last day of our trip. Late that morning, the snow started to fall and continued until two inches had accumulated on the local roads. We had finished having lunch at a restaurant just outside the city, and were heading back on to the highway to make our way to the airport.

Let's just say that we were lucky to get to the airport on time. The corridor we were driving on has the heaviest traffic in all of Alaska, and people routinely drive 70 miles per hour when road conditions are good. The fresh snow failed to inspire a change in behavior on the part of many motorists that day, and people were still driving the same speeds as they had for the previous three months. Wrecks were happening all around us, and the four-lane traffic was reduced to one lane as pileups appeared at every overpass. The local television news that evening reported on the record-setting number of car accidents that took place earlier in the day.

Why didn't people see the snow and adjust their driving accordingly? The answer is that many motorists that day were driving in a state of complacency. Clearly, their minds were set, and three months of normal driving had contributed to a collective inability to adapt to changing conditions. Everyone was thinking subconsciously that winter was over with and they wouldn't have to deal with any more slippery road conditions. This inflexibility in their thinking contributed to extraordinarily dangerous situations on roads all over the city.

COMPLACENCY IN THE WORKPLACE

Complacency is a common occurrence in the workplace. For the purposes of our discussion, complacency is a temporary mindset that occurs when a worker or group of workers is incapable of allowing for alternative outcomes while performing a given task. In other words, a complacent worker believes, perhaps subconsciously, that a job they've done repeatedly will always produce the same result. There are a number of factors that help expand our understanding of complacency. These can be easily remembered by using the acronym C.U.R.B.S:

1. **C**omfortable
2. **U**naware
3. **R**epetition
4. **B**oredom
5. **S**uccess

Comfortable. A complacent worker is a comfortable worker. Being comfortable leads workers to become relaxed while performing a task and stop watching for changes in conditions.

A collective complacency takes place when a work site goes for a long period without an injury. The longer the "winning streak" continues, the stronger the sense of invincibility in the workers on the site. Prolonged success can cause workers to start believing that they will never get hurt, which leads them to become very comfortable. Whether an incident takes place is not a matter of if, but when.

This dynamic is similar to living in a region that is known for seismic activity (earthquakes). The longer that the area goes without an earthquake, the higher the probability for a really strong quake to take place. The lack of activity also leads the residents to lower their guard and stop preparing for the possibility.

Unaware. Complacent workers often fail to consider that for every task you perform, a series of variables has to line up in your favor for you to complete that task successfully. For example, there are multiple variables that can affect your safety when shoveling snow. This could include wet snow that is very heavy, hidden ice patches affecting your footing, or how high you have to lift the snow to dump it. You may have shoveled snow in the same place numerous times in the past, but a variable could change and lead to an injury if your head isn't in the game.

Snow removal is a common outdoor activity during a typical Alaska winter. While my kids and I shovel most of the areas around our house regularly, we have a walkway around the back where we don't bother clearing snow during the winter months. This leaves the path more or less impassable, but we usually work on getting it cleared once Spring comes around. One warm day in April, I was shoveling snow in this area and wasn't thinking of new hazards that could present themselves with the bright sun that was shining.

I had been shoveling this walkway for about an hour, when suddenly a heavy piece of snow and ice slid off our steel roof and landed on a place where I had just been working. This had taken me completely by surprise, and I could have been badly hurt if I had been struck by it. My mind was not looking for changes in variables, which could have led to tragic consequences.

Unawareness of changing variables is a sure sign of complacency. The moment you stop asking "what could go wrong?" is when you have started down a path of putting yourself and your coworkers at risk.

Repetition. Complacency typically occurs after a period of performing a repetitive task. When you carry out a task over and over with the same result every time, your mind can eventually fool you into believing that the outcome will never be different. When you reach this threshold, you stop looking for new information and rely solely on your experience thus far.

In this regard, your brain works similar to web browsing software such as Google Chrome or Internet Explorer. Web browsers incorporate a function known as the "cache," which is space on your computer's hard drive for saving web pages that you have visited. When you return to a website that you have visited in the past, the page that you see on your screen was likely stored in your cache during a previous visit. The browser has taken the page directly from your hard drive, rather than attempting to download it from the internet. This compensates for slow internet connections and makes the browsing experience smoother.

Tasks that we perform over and over are like web pages we visit frequently. The information we need to complete the task has already been stored in our personal cache (experience), so we don't need to go looking for additional data. This works well, provided that no changes take place in the conditions that are critical to task completion.

When changes take place on a web page that is stored in your computer's cache, the browser typically recognizes those changes and downloads the latest version. However, one of the issues with web browsers is that they sometimes fail to update the cache when they should. There could be new information available to be downloaded, but the viewer is not aware of it. The only way to know for sure that you have the latest version of any given web page is to click the browser's "refresh" button.

Complacency is similar to when a browser fails to update the web page in the cache. This is because a complacent worker has stopped acquiring new information. The worker is relying solely on experience and is unable to adjust to changes in conditions that can affect the outcome of the task. The only cure is for the worker to manually "refresh their cache" by questioning their own assumptions and to actively look for vital task-related information.

Boredom. Repetitive tasks can eventually lead to workers lapsing into boredom. This can develop into complacency because the workers' minds start to wander and they think about everything except the task at hand. Workers that have entered this state are very slow to react to changing conditions.

I know a young Army veteran who served multiple tours in Afghanistan. As a squad leader he had many responsibilities, but the most important was keeping his Soldiers sharp and ready to respond if their unit was attacked. This is one of the biggest challenges for non-commissioned officers in the field because service in a war zone often involves endless hours of scanning the landscape for enemy activity.

When nothing happens for a long time, it is easy to get bored and lose your focus.

This is a trap that would befall his machine gunners on humvees and other wheeled vehicles. If they had spent many uneventful hours manning the gun during a patrol, they would often be very slow to respond when the enemy suddenly appeared. Gunners that had lapsed into this state of mind were no longer protectors of their unit; they were now placing themselves and their comrades in extreme danger.

Any worker that performs repetitive tasks can have the same thing happen to them. Boredom breeds complacency, which causes a worker to be slow in responding to a change in conditions. More often than not, this leads to a very different outcome from what the worker was expecting.

Success. Success is a major contributor to complacency. How many times have you heard a coworker tell you that "they have always done it this way?" The assumption behind this statement is that because their technique always worked in the past, it will continue to work in the future. It should also be noted that just because their way has worked, it doesn't mean that it is the best way to do it.

Success serves to embolden workers to take progressively higher risks. Risk taking plays out as shortcuts used in an effort to save time and/or effort. The first time a worker attempts a shortcut, they may be fearful because they don't know for sure whether it will work. If they complete the task and nothing bad happens, the fear factor starts to diminish and the worker will be more than willing to use the shortcut again.

Pulling off a shortcut is brain candy. We feel smart when we devise shortcuts and they appear to work; certainly smarter than those who came up with the procedure we were supposed to follow. Continued success leads to a further reduction of fear and an increase in carelessness. As long as the shortcut works, the worker will continue on a downward spiral of putting themselves and their coworkers at risk. The inevitable result is that eventually the shortcut fails, which could result in someone getting hurt or killed.

HOW EXPERIENCE WORKS AGAINST YOU

One would expect that as a worker gains experience, they would become progressively safer. An experienced worker should have better knowledge of what the hazards are when performing a task and therefore act with appropriate caution.

In reality, it often works exactly the opposite; the more experience you have can make it that much more likely that you will get hurt or killed while performing that task. This is because experience can be a key contributor to complacency.

A tragic example of how complacency kills took place on November 18, 2013, when a group of contract electricians were finishing work on an equipment installation at a limestone quarry in northwestern Kentucky.[5] The scope of their project was to install two submersible pumps and the associated control gear that would supply river water for washing crushed limestone. The pumps were powered by high-voltage electricity, and generated 450 horsepower each. Power for each pump was supplied by a Motor Control Center (MCC), which, in turn, was controlled by a low-voltage Programmable Logic Controller (PLC).

The job had been in construction phase for 12 weeks, and had reached the point where it was ready for commissioning. The work day started with a safety meeting at 7:00 a.m., and the electricians were notified by their foreman that the equipment would be powered up for the first time that day. The foreman, himself, was a highly experienced electrician with 14 years in the trade, and he had been on this particular job from its inception.

As work got underway, the electricians completed the connections to the river pumps, while the foreman proceeded to connect the cables to the feed transformer for the MCCs. This phase was complete at 11:40 a.m., and the power to the equipment was turned on shortly thereafter. Everything had gone well so far that day, and the group went to lunch at 12:00 noon.

When they came back from lunch, two electricians went to work to complete the wiring for the PLC. An inspection by the foreman revealed that there were two more low-voltage wires that would have to be installed between the PLC and the MCC. While the two electricians continued their work at the PLC, the foreman opened the door of the MCC enclosure (just five feet away) to finish the last two connections. The door of the MCC swung outward towards the PLC, so the electricians couldn't see what the foreman was doing as he worked.

Shortly thereafter, the foreman fell backwards against the wall of the building and then crumpled to the floor. The electricians working at the PLC rushed to his aid,

finding him unconscious and unresponsive. Mine personnel applied CPR and an Automatic External Defibrillator
(AED), and the foreman was eventually medevaced to a
hospital where he died four days later.

The incident investigation determined two contributing factors to the foreman's death:

1. The MCC electrical circuit had not been de-ener-
   gized prior to work being performed on it. This included the circuit breaker in the MCC enclosure as
   well as the circuit that supplied power to the MCC.
2. The MCC electrical circuit had not been locked
   out/tagged out, and had not been tested to verify
   de-energization.

How does an electrician with 14 years of experience die by
electrocution? One factor to consider is that prior to that
fateful day, the project had been in construction phase for
12 weeks. During that time, none of the circuits they were
working on had power applied to them. In all likelihood,
the electricians didn't wear PPE to protect themselves from
electrical shock, and lockout/tagout/tryout procedures
weren't being used.

Then, one variable changed.

The foreman was aware that the circuit was energized. He told the men on his crew that the circuit was going to be energized, and he had ordered it turned on. However, he had become so comfortable with the way they had gone about things that his work routine failed to adjust. Complacency had taken hold, and changes in variables were ignored.

CHANGE IT UP

No one is exempt from the effects of complacency. It should be noted, however, that the workers who are in the most trouble are those who aren't struggling with it. In other words, keeping yourself and your coworkers safe implies that you are continually questioning whether you have acquired some level of complacency.

Assessing your personal complacency level is an act of discipline, and requires a worker to be able to think about their own thinking. Nobody can do this for you; you need to question everything you do and look for trouble spots. Thinking about complacency in these terms may reveal problem areas that you hadn't thought about before.

We can all learn something about combating complacency from Costco Wholesale, the Seattle-based retail warehouse giant. Anyone that has shopped regularly at a Costco store knows that the items in the store don't stay in the same place for very long. This can present a challenge for the shopper because when you come into the store looking for a particular item, it will likely have been moved from where it was the last time you visited.

Costco's marketing strategy is based on preventing the shopper from acquiring a set in their thinking regarding where certain products are located. That means that you spend more time in the store than you initially intended, and you view more items than you would have if you were able to go straight to what you wanted. This "complacency busting" works extremely well for revenue generation. My personal experience is that you buy more stuff than you wanted, and it is rare for me to leave the store without spending at least one hundred dollars!

The point is this: we all need to be doing the same thing with our work environments. What are the tasks that we do over and over again? Do a self-audit to pinpoint the tasks you do that could foster complacency, then get creative about making a change.

Some simple suggestions for "changing it up" include:

1. As a heavy equipment operator, you realize that you always walk clockwise around a piece of machinery when doing a pre-operation inspection. Try walking around counter-clockwise and see if you observe anything different.

2. You have an inspection form to fill out daily, and you see that it has become an exercise in "checking the boxes." Instead of going from top to bottom on the form, try starting at the bottom and working your way up (if it can be done safely).

3. Your department determines that it's always the same people that fill out work permit forms. Reassign this task to different people in an effort to see the work environment through a different set of eyes.

4. Stop to think as you are drawing close to finishing a job, especially one that has gone on for some time. Remind yourself that it is easy to get into a rush as you near completion, and that you are even less likely to recognize changes in variables under these conditions.

Now is the time to address trouble spots in your work environment that can lead to complacency. Think carefully about where you need to make improvements on this front, then share what you've learned with your coworkers. This could inspire others to do their own self-audits, and then make changes to avoid the dangers of complacency.

—◊—

Principle #9: The war on
complacency is never won.

Question to Consider: Are you struggling
with complacency? If not, why not?

—◊—

11

Why supervisors die

"Pride deafens us to the advice or warnings of those around us."

- JOHN C. MAXWELL

There are certain aspects of safety that are, quite frankly, puzzling. One of the "safety paradoxes" that we've already explored is how more experience can serve to make you more likely to get hurt or killed on the job. At first glance, this doesn't make sense because we like to believe that an experienced worker is more aware of workplace hazards and will do everything they can to avoid them. The reality, however, is that more experience can lead to complacency, which puts both individuals and their co-workers at greater risk.

Another phenomenon that is difficult to understand is that while any worker could potentially get injured, supervisors can be at greater risk. This is the opposite of what one would expect. Some workers in supervisory roles accepted those positions because they wanted to do less physically demanding work. They may have hoped to reduce their risk of getting injured and, thereby, extend their careers. Some supervisors weren't given a choice; an injury they suffered may have put them in a position where a supervisory role is their only option. Either way, they may not be any safer if their mindset is at odds with their personal safety goals.

The U.S. Mine Safety and Health Administration (MSHA) is well aware of these issues because there have been periods where supervisors have been disproportionately represented in mine fatalities. On average, there is typically one supervisor for 10 workers on a mine site. Based on that ratio, one could expect that supervisors would represent 10% or less of fatalities that occur. However, the statistics recorded from October 2013 to August 2014 were shocking by any measure. Of 25 fatalities that took place in metal/nonmetal mines during that period, 8 were supervisors (over 30%).[6] This disturbing statistic flies in the face of conventional wisdom, and prompted MSHA to place a special emphasis on safety-related training for supervisory personnel.

You would think that supervisors would be the least likely to get hurt on the job. They are often the most experienced individuals on a work site, and have a depth of knowledge that should keep them out of trouble. Many supervisors spend at least part of their day in an office, away from the hazards they would have to deal with if they were back at their old jobs. Despite this, there are a number of factors that can put a supervisor at risk when they venture into the field:

1. Distractions
2. Atrophy
3. Unawareness
4. Complacency
5. Fear
6. Ego

Any one of these factors can lead to a supervisor being hurt or killed on the job. It is worth your time to take a more careful look at each of these, and consider whether they may be impacting the safety of you and your coworkers.

Distractions. Most supervisors will tell you that they have a lot more to take care of in their current jobs than they did when they were "on the floor." Now, they are worrying about managing a number of projects instead of just taking care of their own. Beyond that, they often have administrative duties that pull them away from paying attention to their workers in the field.

A typical supervisor deals with a steady stream of phone calls, email, and even radio messages. When they go to the field with a specific purpose in mind, a sudden radio call can get them turned in a different direction. This can serve to knock them off their stride and create circumstances that impact their safety as well as those around them. Among the victims of distractions is situational awareness. Supervisors that arrive at a job site may have a number of other things on their mind, and these can lead to them being unable to focus on critical pieces of information that they need to stay safe.

Atrophy. When a worker accepts a position as a supervisor, they enter into a world that is quite different from what they had known in the past. The day-to-day routine of their new job requires a very different skill set, and they have less exposure to the tasks they may have been really good at in their previous role.

While a newly-minted supervisor will be busy practicing the new tasks they are responsible for (such as work on a computer), there can be an associated deterioration of their field skills. In other words, they're going to "get rusty." This effect is less pronounced with working foremen that spend the majority of their time alongside the other workers on the job. However, a more rapid decay takes place as the supervisor progresses up the ladder and spends less and less time in the field.

To be clear, getting rusty is a natural occurrence when you haven't performed a task in some time. Where supervisors get into trouble is when they want to show the world that "they've still got it" when they may not. Self-awareness is key; every supervisor needs to know their limitations and act accordingly. Those who feel the need to prove themselves are treading on thin ice and could put themselves and their workers in jeopardy.

I once heard a supervisor tell the story of a foreman who wasn't satisfied with the performance of one of his equipment operators. He instructed the operator to get out of the machine so he could "show him how it was done." Shortly thereafter, the foreman had a wreck, proving to those who witnessed the ordeal that he really didn't know what he was doing after all. If the foreman's objective was to correct a deficiency in his operator's methods, a surer path would have been to acknowledge that he hadn't run a machine in a long time and to recommend that training be provided by an expert operator.

Unawareness. Distractions combined with an atrophy of field skills can cause a supervisor to lack awareness of hazards in the workplace. Supervisors that get killed in the field were often recent arrivals at that particular job. Why were they there in the first place? Typically, it is because the job is stopped and the pressure is on to get it going again. The supervisor has been summoned, and they arrive at the site having been redirected from a different concern. They may have a number of other problems they are dealing with, so the priority is to get this one taken care of as quickly as possible. Under these circumstances, it is easy to develop a case of "tunnel vision" and overlook hazards that are obvious to the other workers on the job.

Being away from the field for an extended period may have led to the supervisor losing touch with the hazards that are all too familiar to their workers. Ironically, everyone else could be thinking that because they are a supervisor, they should know what the pitfalls are. This type of situation becomes more dangerous when the supervisor doesn't take the time to ask for a briefing on the hazards that exist in that area.

One last possibility: a supervisor may have been hired into their current position without any previous field experience. Self-awareness and humility are critical in this situation; if the supervisor is aware of their own lack of knowledge, they must rely on the people that work for them for information necessary to stay safe.

Complacency. As discussed in Chapter 10, complacency is borne of doing a job repetitively, to the point that you get comfortable with the way you do it. You may be doing it in an unsafe manner, but you've gotten away with it so many times that you don't think anything could ever go wrong. As a result, you no longer keep an eye out for hazards or changing conditions.

Supervisors are not exempt from this dynamic. They can exhibit complacency when they attempt to perform a task that they used to do all the time, but have not done in recent years because their job duties have changed. Their assumption is that the way they did it in the past should work just as well now. The supervisor could be out-of-practice, and may have forgotten important details. Beyond that, they could overestimate their body's strength and flexibility to the point that they injure themselves.

Complacency is a contributing factor in many aviation incidents, and when they happen, supervisors are often at the focal point. On June 4, 2015, a group of four single-engine aircraft was being prepared for a cross-country instructional flight at an airstrip located in Alaska's Wrangell-St. Elias National Park.[7] The instructor, a retired U.S. Air Force pilot, was highly qualified with a total of 12,000 hours of flight time in a variety of aircraft. The four propeller-driven Piper Super Cubs were parked slightly staggered in a wingtip-to-wingtip formation while they were being loaded with gear. However, the engines of all four aircraft were started and allowed to idle unattended to defend against clouds of mosquitoes that surrounded the instructor and his three students.

The instructor was loading gear on the right side of one of the Super Cubs, when he noticed that the unoccupied aircraft to the immediate left was moving forward. He attempted to intercept the moving aircraft by running around the front of the plane he was loading, only to be killed when he was struck three times by his own plane's propeller. According to the National Transportation Safety Board's final report, he had likely attempted to cut directly in front of the plane he was loading to avoid the spinning propeller of the moving plane.

The instructor was a highly experienced aviator. He had likely walked in front of a parked Piper Super Cub many times when the plane's engine was shut off. Presumably, he had given the order to have the engines idling while the planes were being loaded. However, this particular time, he failed to take into account that his own plane's engine was running when he attempted to stop the moving plane. Complacency was a contributing factor in his death.

Fear. Workers do not always feel that their supervisors are approachable. They may fear retribution or a vendetta against them if they identify a safety concern and it is not received well. If the supervisor is embarrassed or angered by an observation or suggestion, it could lead to them lashing out at the worker. A vindictive supervisor may decide to write a negative evaluation, assign less than desirable work assignments, or deny pay upgrades to the worker. Just the perception that this could happen may lead many workers to keep their safety concerns to themselves.

Supervisors need to encourage their people to talk to them, to eliminate hesitation when a worker observes a hazard that the supervisor may not see. A supervisor should also ask themselves whether they are approachable, and to look for indications that their subordinates feel free to communicate their concerns.

We all need to be disciplined about how we respond to those who approach us with safety concerns. Negative feedback can lead the giver of a safety concern to decide that they won't bother trying that again because it won't do any good and may even work against them. Always thank a person who has the moral courage to offer you a safety concern, even if they are misinformed. Be sure to take advantage of "teachable moments" and take the time to talk it out with them.

Ego. A potential threat to a supervisor's personal safety is ego. Some supervisors are reluctant to ask for help, and try to put up a front that suggests they know more than they do. They could be holding tightly to the following presuppositions:

As a supervisor, I should know everything.
I can't let anyone know that I don't know everything.

Should a supervisor know everything? If you feel this way, it's time to get a new perspective. First off, it isn't even possible. Effective supervisors are fully aware that they will always need new information, and that much of it will come from listening to those they are responsible for. Taking counsel from the people that work for you builds morale and increases their willingness to warn you of safety hazards in the field.

Inexperienced supervisors may be more susceptible to these types of insecurities. They could be afraid that they will be considered underqualified or lose respect if they don't know everything there is to know about their job. Over time, supervisors often get over this and openly rely on their subordinates to help make decisions. The supervisor that is putting up a front can get into trouble safety-wise because they aren't receptive to feedback from the other workers on the site. Questions from subordinates may be interpreted as challenges to their authority, and could serve to steel their will to do it their way - despite the objections of others.

There will always be supervisors who object to the idea of letting their workers know that they need help of any kind. What they may not realize is how much they increase their personal risk when they hold to that position. Supervisors are human, and they are subject to the same safety principles that apply to every other worker.

Ego can rear its ugly head in another way, one where good intentions can get a supervisor hurt or killed. Sometimes there are tasks that everyone recognizes as being risky, and the supervisor insists that they be the one to perform the job to keep their workers out of harm's way. It is commendable that the supervisor's protective instincts are alive and well, but their ego has messaged their subordinates that they are not subject to the same hazards as everyone else. If the job is that risky, why is it being done in the first place?

A supervisor that is willing to assume elevated risk to keep other workers safe is usually driven by a desire to meet a deadline. A job that hazardous should not be performed at all, and anyone who decides to do it anyway is more intent on getting it done quickly rather than staying safe. They could be justifying their approach by saying that their first concern is the safety of their subordinates, but this doesn't make the job any less dangerous.

Honestly analyzing your own thinking is the only real solution to situations like this. Ask yourself the following questions:

1. Why are you willing to assume inappropriate risk to get the job done?
2. Is your ego overcoming your common sense?

THE SUPERVISOR SETS THE TONE

Supervisors can be subject to higher risk on the job site than any of the other workers. This can happen for a number of reasons, but the supervisors themselves have the most control over how these play out. If you are a supervisor, you need to be proactive in your efforts to avoid becoming another statistic. You must talk to those who report to you and let them know that you need their help to stay safe. At the same time, you need to work on enhancing your approachability. Do you put down the people that work for you, especially in the presence of others? How are you at soliciting and then acting on suggestions from your employees? Do you give your employees credit for good ideas that they contribute? Finally, how do you react when you make a mistake? Do you try to cover it up and make like it never happened, or do you own it? Everyone already knows that you're human, and will view you as more approachable when you are willing to admit it.

Supervisors, just like all other workers, need to gain awareness of their own thinking. They are subject to complacency and a self-imposed sense of urgency the same as everyone else. At the same time, the impacts of these phenomena are magnified when experienced by supervisors. To coin a phrase, "with great power, comes great responsibility." As a supervisor, you have the power to set the tone on your crew; partner with them to build a safety culture that doesn't accept compromise.

Principle #10: Supervisors need
everyone's help to stay safe.

Question to Consider: Supervisors - are
you approachable? How do you know?

12

Counting the costs

"Integrity is doing the right thing, even when no one is watching."

- C.S. LEWIS

Risk is inherent in everything we do. Whether at work or at home, we assume some level of risk in every activity we engage in. In some cases, we "look before we leap" and think carefully about the risks beforehand. However, there are other situations where we dive right in without giving it a second thought.

Sound business practice is based on the concept of risk versus reward. Before putting money into a business venture, a prudent investor will assess the risk of losing their money if things go wrong. If the risk is low, a modest return on the investment may be acceptable. However, riskier investments require higher potential returns. You could lose it all, but if you win, you win big.

This is the basic idea behind bond ratings. Companies that sell bonds to finance their operations will receive a credit rating from an agency such as Moody's or Standard and Poor's. If the rating agency assesses the risk of defaulting on a bond obligation to be low, they will assign the company a higher credit rating. This means that the company will pay a lower interest rate on their bonds, and the buyers of the bonds receive a lower return. Conversely, companies that have less stable financial outlooks will receive lower credit ratings, and buyers of their bonds will receive a higher interest rate to compensate for the increased risk.

In regards to safety, we all need to conduct ourselves as if we are in business. First, we need to objectively assess the risks prior to engaging in any activity. Beyond that, we need an awareness of the true value of the rewards we will receive for taking the risks. Most employees would be shocked to realize that the rewards they are striving for are not nearly as valuable as they first thought.

A classic example of this is "End of Shift Syndrome." A high percentage of incidents take place in the last hour of an employee's shift because they are focusing on going home and are less willing to take the time to do the job right. Self-imposed sense of urgency looms large during this period, and the employee places a higher value on getting the job done before the end of the work day. The perceived reward increases the employee's risk tolerance, making it more likely that an incident will take place. If an incident does occur, the notion of getting home on time is out the window because the employee is now subject to an investigation and possible medical treatment if they or a coworker was injured. Now, the value of the reward (getting home on time) has plunged, and the risk/reward ratio has fallen out of balance. What used to be a good idea has now become "what was I thinking?"

While we tend to overestimate the rewards for risky behaviors, we also discount the risks and what it could cost us if things go wrong. Again, we would all be better off if we treated safety as if it were a business proposition.

BUSINESS AND SAFETY

Most companies approach safety from a business perspective. They know that doing what they can to prevent incidents will cost them up front. However, these costs are known and can be built into a business plan. In other words, being proactive on safety gives the company a degree of cost certainty. Cost certainty is the "holy grail" of the business world. The idea is to reduce risk by eliminating the unknown. Any line item on the balance sheet that cannot be predicted is a threat to the business plan and, therefore, to the company itself.

One alternative is to do little or nothing to address safety and hope for the best. This approach is not acceptable in the world of business because there is no telling how much it will cost when incidents take place. Incidents are unknowns; the company can't know for sure how many they will have, or their severity. The only realistic approach is to set goals and then do everything possible to prevent incidents from taking place.

We all strive for cost certainty. This is one of the reasons that people live in fear of taking their car to a mechanic. They know there is something wrong with their car and they can't fix it themselves. However, they don't know what it is going to cost them, or how they will pay for it if it turns into a major repair. One of my personal experiences with this is our home internet plan that provided us with 250 gigabytes of data per month, then charged $2 for each gigabyte we went over our limit. If it were only my wife and me, we wouldn't have a problem. However, my eldest son is renowned for burning up data and represented a threat to the family budget. I have been at my internet provider's customer service desk more than once, looking for ways to prevent constant overages. I was relieved when they introduced their "No Worries" plan that sold us a certain amount of data, but only slowed down our connection if we were to exceed the limit. Even in the world of personal finance, cost certainty is everything.

You should learn to think about safety the same way your employer does. First, every employee needs to be aware that there is no upper limit on what it could cost them to get injured. Some may fool themselves into believing that there are no personal costs...but they are horribly wrong. The potential financial, physical, and emotional toll of getting hurt cannot be measured, making it an unknown in your personal budget. Yes, an injury you suffer will cost your employer a lot of money, but they will write a check and be done with it. You, on the other hand, could potentially pay for the rest of your living days.

WHAT AN INJURY WILL COST YOU

Just like your employer, an employee will incur direct and indirect costs when they get injured. Direct costs are factors that leave the employee with less money in their pocket. Here are two for your consideration:

Reduced income. While you could collect a disability income while you recover, this is typically a good deal less than what you would take in if you were working. This is fixed income because you can't work overtime and there aren't likely to be any safety bonuses paid out when you get hurt.

Medical bills. Depending on whether you were injured at work or off-site, you may have deductibles and copays related to your medical treatment. You could also have part or all of your claim rejected by the insurance company.

A mechanic I know suffered two back injuries while working in the oil and gas industry. His initial injury took place when he was installing a large electric motor. While the motor was being moved into place, it suddenly started to roll off the cart it was sitting on. He attempted to stop it from falling, hurting his back in the process. He partially recovered from this injury, but had to take a job as a supervisor because he wasn't able to safely lift sufficient weight to go back to his job as a mechanic. Not long after returning to work, he suffered a second back injury when he assisted another employee with lifting some heavy batteries. He hasn't been able to work since his second injury, and he and his family have now been living on long-term disability payments for years. His income since he was injured has been a great deal less than what he would have made if he was working full-time. To make matters worse, he was forced to engage in a prolonged battle with the insurance company over who was going to pay for another back surgery and other medical care related to his injury.

While an injury can cost an employee a lot of money, these costs are still small potatoes relative to the indirect costs. The employee's indirect costs can't be quantified in terms of dollars and cents. However, they have a much greater impact on the employee, their family, and their friends. They can also be described as cascading liabilities because any one of these will affect some or all of the others.

Diminished productivity. Most employees want to feel as though they are making a contribution when they are at work. Certainly, we all need our jobs to earn a living, but the sense of accomplishment most of us get from having done a solid day's work forms an important component of our identity. Those who return to work after recovering from an injury are sometimes unable to perform their duties at the same level that they did before. They may work more slowly, and there may be some tasks that they can't do at all. The employee may feel as though they aren't earning their keep, which could also lead to a reduction in their self-esteem.

Loss of quality time. Injuries can leave the employee unable to participate in activities that they used to enjoy with family and friends. Recreation could be an area of their life that is most greatly impacted by an injury. The loss of an ability to play hockey, go backpacking, or participate in other sports could be devastating, and may serve to reinforce feelings of inadequacy and isolation. This puts additional stress on relationships with the people that are closest to them.

Physical pain and suffering. The pain that results from a minor injury could be short-term. However, more serious injuries could leave the employee with chronic pain and the potential to develop a dependence on painkillers.

Even if the employee recovers from the physical injury, an addiction can live on with another set of consequences to go along with it.

Mental distress. A majority of active people cannot stand being stuck in the house while they recover from an injury. An inability to work off excess energy can drive most people crazy. Mind-numbing boredom and sleepless nights dominate their existence if they don't find a way to distract themselves.

You've likely heard the phrase, "You are your own worst critic." An injury can leave the employee with a lot of spare time during their recovery period, and a common path is for their mind to turn on itself. Self-accusation is a common byproduct of a workplace injury, even if it was someone else's fault. The employee's anguish only gets worse when it was their own actions that resulted in themselves and/or a coworker getting injured. Intense guilt can lead to self-destructive behaviors such as drug and alcohol abuse, which compounds the suffering of the employee and those around them.

Alienation. Recovery from an injury can put tremendous pressure on relationships. A fellow I know tells the story of a welder he worked with who was injured on the job and never fully recovered. He was working behind a service truck, when suddenly a welding gas bottle came loose and fell off the truck bed. Rather than standing back and allowing it to hit the ground, the welder caught the heavy bottle in his arms, wrenching his back in the process. While he did return to work after his back injury, a second injury to his knee left him semi-disabled. This time he was injured to the extent that he couldn't work, and eventually became addicted to painkillers. To support his habit, he resorted to petty theft, eventually becoming alienated from almost every person that had been close to him. This was especially heartbreaking to watch because his parents were respected members of the community whose boy had been raised with a different set of values.

There is no dollar value that can be attached to the loss suffered by the welder. The people closest to him also paid a terrible price for his injury. His story only reinforces the fact that the indirect costs to the employee for a workplace injury are far more punishing than the money they lose.

HOW SHOULD WE THEN LIVE?
Depending on your mindset, safety can be a hassle. Getting the right equipment, filling out the permit paperwork, and

following the proper procedures often seems to slow down a project. Shortcuts, on the other hand, can be incredibly tempting.

I could get this done in a few minutes if I just …

Employees that are willing to accept inappropriate risk to get a job done have talked themselves into believing that the rewards are greater than they really are. If they step back and think about it, they will often realize that the "pot of gold" they are striving for is an illusion and there is no way to justify the risks.

You make decisions daily as to whether you're going to partner with your employer's safety program. So, no matter what regulations and procedures are put into place, it is still up to you to decide if you are going to follow suit. What will motivate you to make the right decision?

Look at the following list and decide for yourself which is most important to you:

1. **Keeping your job** - if you get caught violating safety rules, you could get fired.
2. **Keeping your coworkers safe** - taking shortcuts can put your coworkers and their families at risk.

3. **Taking care of your family** - your own family will suffer immeasurable consequences if you are injured or killed.
4. **Staying injury-free** - workplace injuries could impact your life long-term, even after your work career is over.

We generally don't stop to think about the possible consequences when we take shortcuts. More often than not, our focus is on the here and now and our inner desire to get this job done as quickly as possible.

A recurring theme of this book has been to take a moment and consider carefully both the risks and the rewards. I encourage you to consider the four factors listed above as part of your thought process when you are making safety decisions.

Take care of yourselves, people.

Ten Principles of Safety

Principle #1 - You aren't doing yourself or your employer any favors when you take shortcuts.

Principle #2 - For your own sake, you are your brother's keeper.

Principle #3 - A true student of safety takes responsibility for their own learning.

Principle #4 - Always offer to help when delivering a safety concern.

Principle #5 - The benefit of the doubt will lead you to a safer solution *every time*.

Principle #6 - Your personal safety goals become more achievable when you contribute to the safety of others.

Principle #7 - Deadlines are important, but not more important than safety.

Principle #8 - Safety has no hierarchy.

Principle #9 - The war on complacency is never won.

Principle #10 - Supervisors need everyone's help to stay safe.

Endnotes

1. Sinclair, Upton. *The Jungle.* A public domain book, 1906.

2. "OSHA's $afety Pays Program." *www.osha.gov* United States Department of Labor. Web. Accessed 12 Aug 2017

3. "Success Stories and Case Studies: The Great American Ballpark." *www.osha.gov* United States Department of Labor. Web. Accessed 13 Aug 2017

4. Waters, Roger. "Another Brick in the Wall (Part 2). *The Wall.* Columbia Records. 1979. LP.

5. "Report of Investigation: MAI-2013-18." *www.msha.gov* United States Department of Labor. Web. Accessed 14 Aug 2017.

6. Nadzadi, George. "Q2-14-training-summit." *www. msha.gov* United States Department of Labor. August 2014. PowerPoint presentation.

7. "Aviation Accident Final Report: ANC15LA035." *www.ntsb.gov* National Transportation Safety Board. June 2015. PDF. Accessed 14 Aug 2017.

About the Author

John Anthony (Tony) Martin has worked for 33 years in industry and post-secondary education. His career began with a heavy duty equipment mechanic apprenticeship in Canada. Years later, he earned an A.A.S. in Diesel Technology and a B.S. in Technology Education from the University of Alaska.

Tony's teaching career began at Ilisagvik College in Barrow, Alaska (now Utqiagvik). He went on to become a faculty member at the University of Alaska Southeast in Juneau, where he was promoted to full professor. Tony has been a contributing editor for Motor Age magazine since 2006, and continues to write about automotive and diesel technology topics.

While he currently works as a trainer in the mining industry, he has operated a mobile equipment repair business, and worked in a chemical plant, a liquefied natural gas plant, refineries, and offshore oil platforms. Each of these settings has provided experiences that fueled the perspective he shares in this book.

Tony has lived in Alaska for over 25 years, where he and his wife Lara have raised five children.

Tony can be contacted by email at jatonymartin@gmail.com

Made in the USA
Lexington, KY
16 September 2019